from *Gay Testaments:*
Old and New

Which is more dear: Fame or health?
Which is more valuable: Health or wealth?
Which is more baneful: Gain or loss?
Excessive love is bound to cause great expense.

—Lao Tzu

Sooner murder an infant in its cradle than nurse unacted desires.

—William Blake

The king of the gods once loved a Trojan boy
Named Ganymede...

—Ovid

Some swore he was a maid in man's attire,
For in his looks were all that men desire...

— Christopher Marlowe

Bearded Callistratus married rugged Afer in the usual form
in which a virgin marries a husband. The torches shone in front,
the wedding veil covered his face, and you, Thalassus, you
did not lack your words. Even the dowry was declared. Are
you still not satisfied, Rome? Are you waiting for him to give
birth?

—Martial

Thetis brought to the beach her gifts from the god of fire. She
found her dear son lying beside Patróklos, wailing, while his
men stood by in tears around him....
     "I shall not forget him while I can keep my feet among
the living. If in the dead world they forget the dead, I say there,
too, I shall remember him, ... No burden like this grief will
come a second time upon my heart, while I remain among the
living...."

—Homer

When [David] had finished speaking to Saul, the soul of Jonathan was knit to the soul of David, and Jonathan loved him as his own soul... Then Jonathan made a covenant with David, because he loved him as his own soul.

—*The Book of Samuel*

Devouring Time...
      ...I forbid thee one most heinous crime;
O, carve not with thy hours my love's fair brow,
Nor draw no lines there with thy antique pen;
Him in his course untainted do allow
For beauty's pattern to succeeding men....

—*Shakespeare*

... A new commandment I give to you, that you love one another. By this all men will know that you are my disciples, if you have love for one another....This is my commandment, that you love one another as I have loved you. ...

—*The Book of John*

The artist is the creator of beautiful things....The world is made by the singer for the dreamer.

—*Oscar Wilde*

You pluck your chest and your shins and your arms, and your shaven cock is ringed with short hairs. This, Labienus, you do for your mistress' sake, as everybody knows. For whose sake, Labienus, do you depilate your ass?

—*Martial*

As the caterpillar chooses the fairest leaf to lay her eggs on, so the priest lays his curse on the fairest joys....

—*William Blake*

To a Boy:...Pray, what greatness is there in being, before you depart from life, a chaste corpse? Garland yourself with flowers before you wither away...

—*Philostratus*

GAY
TESTAMENTS
Old and New

GAY
TESTAMENTS
Old and New

Compiled and edited by
BELA DORNON

Wind-Up Publications
San Diego, California

Kind acknowledgment is made for permission to reprint the following :

The Complete Kama Sutra: The First Unabridged Modern Translation of The Classic Indian Text by Vatsyayana, translation by Alain Daniélou © 1994, an imprint of Inner Traditions, reprinted by permission of Park Street Press. *Dancing With Siva*, Satguru Sivaya Subramuniyaswami, reprinted by the very kind permission of the Himalayan Academy. *The Guiding Light of Lao-Tzu: A New Translation and Commentary on the Tao Teh Ching*, Henry Wei, reprinted by the very kind permission of Quest Books. *The Iliad*, translated by Robert Fitzgerald, reprinted by permission of Doubleday Dell Bantam. *The Letters of Alcipron, Aelian, and Philostratus*, with an English translation by Allen Rogers Benner, reprinted by the very kind permission of Harvard University Press. *Martial: Epigrams*, edited and translated by D. R. Shackleton Bailey, in three volumes, reprinted by the very kind permission of Harvard University Press. *Ovid: Metamorphoses*, translated by Rolfe Humphries, reprinted by permission of Indiana University Press. *A Return To Love*, Marianne Williamson, reprinted by permission of HarperCollins. *Messages from Michael* by Chelsea Quinn Yarbro, reprinted by permission of Berkley Books. Selections from *The Revised Standard Version of the Bible*© 1946, 1952, 1971 by the Division of Christian Educational of the National Council of the Churches of Christ USA, used by permission.

Gay Testaments: Old and New © 1998 Wind-Up Publications.
ISBN: 0-9659828-6-6
Library of Congress Catalog Card Number 97-90960

Wind-Up Publications
http://members.home.net/antinuous

2828 University Avenue #103-121
San Diego, California 92104
voice mail (619) 497-5081
antinuous@home.net

Cover art: second century Roman sculpture of Antinuous

With all my love,
for my husband,
Phil

TABLE OF CONTENTS

Introduction

Gay Testaments: Old and New is a book for gay men, and for our friends.

My intention in writing this book is to provide a collection of carefully edited writings for and about gay men that gives a sense of our various historical and cultural identities, and a sampling of diverse positive philosophical attitudes towards gay men.

I grew up believing that I was the only one like me. Even though the kids in school had called me "faggot" since I was nine years old, I didn't find out what that word meant until I was fourteen. In my little town library, there were absolutely no books whatsoever that talked about gay people. I know, because I looked very carefully. Being a bookworm, I naturally started to look in bookstores; pretty soon I discovered David R. Rueben's *Everything You Always Wanted To Know About Sex, But Were Afraid To Ask*, and *The Joy of Sex* by Alex Comfort. There, for the very first time, I encountered the concept of men loving other men. True, the authors seemed embarrassed and unhappy about the idea, but at least it was a start. About the same time, I also began to discover evidence of gay men in magazines and small newspapers.

But even though I learned fairly early on that there were lots of gay men in the world, I still had no idea that there were any famous gay men in the past, or that gay men had been the subjects of great literature and art, or that there were entire civilizations which held men loving men in high regard. Luckily for me, I was and still am a bookworm. Reading was generally encouraged in my mother's home, and it was reading which eventually proved my salvation…

Growing up in a fundamentalist Christian religion, my church taught me that it was dangerous to read books which disagreed with or criticized our faith in any way. The Devil, they taught, could deceive me and lead me away from my faith if I read certain books. Over and over I heard church members say that a "liberal education" (by which they meant any exposure to non-Christian ideas) would almost surely result in a loss of faith. Years of Sunday school brainwashing drew a glowing magic circle around my faith: inside all was safety, warmth and the Church's teachings; outside lurked reason and logic— waiting to lead me into darkness and the absolute zero of unbelief.

The first place I looked for information about gay men was, naturally, in the Bible. What I found written there confused me and filled me with dread. Paul wrote about men loving men as though it were a horrible disease; the old Jewish laws at the beginning of the Bible thundered words like "abomination" and "unclean"; believing these terrible words to be the *Word of God*, I almost despaired. Then I discovered the story of Jonathan and David, and it seemed to me that they were lovers! Timidly, I asked my fellow church members if this could be so; they all angrily declared that any notion that the two men loved each other "that way" was a horrible and evil lie of Satan! In the face of such universal condemnation and intimidation, I decided that my elders must know better than I did. And so, for years I lay in a dark prison of ignorance and faith, using reason to defend and prop up my beliefs, rather than as a tool to search for the truth.

But over the years, I also read books which augmented, challenged, contradicted, and eventually transformed my ignorant faith. It started more than fifteen years ago with a charming little paperback called *Holy Blood, Holy Grail.* The premise of the book was simple, yet explosive: Jesus fled Palestine after the "resurrection", and lived in France with his wife and their children. Most of the history of the Christian church presented in that book was unknown to me, and it started me wondering. Then in college I read Homer's *Odyssey,* and seven years after, the *Iliad.* I also read William Blake's *The Marriage of Heaven and Hell* in college, and after many years, began to understand a little of what Blake was saying in that strange eighteenth-century graphic work.

By the beginning of the nineties, I was ready to tackle more difficult ideas. My genetic father urged me to read *Messages From Michael*, which proposes a system of spiritual evolution through voluntary reincarnation. This led me to the *Tao Teh Ching*, China's marvelous mental finger puzzle. By this time, the sails of my old simple faith lay on their broken mast in tatters; the rudder was long gone, and great holes had been slammed into the hull. But it was not until 1993, when I first began to read Plato's *Symposium on Love* and *Phaedo* that the last vestiges of the old wreck sank beneath the waves forever. Along the way, Alain Danielou's *Siva and Dionysis* revealed a whole new series of interesting connections between the Greeks and the Indian sub-continent. I then examined that same author's translation of the *Kama Sutra*, finding a message regarding the normalcy and naturalness of gay people. *Dancing with Shiva* increased my exposure to the world's oldest religion, the Hindu faith.

These texts, and many others, gave me a profound sense of comfort: I stopped seeing myself as a sinful creature in need of redemption, and started to see myself as a whole being in a complex world. I began to believe in the doctrine of personal choice, rather than personal salvation, in the idea that everything that I am and do is the result of my own choice. Far from being a degenerate, sinful, unacceptable sub-human, as the Christians had wanted me to see myself, I beheld myself as an organic part of the physical and spiritual universe in which I existed, with a part to play in the unfolding history of my kind. My education continued as I discovered Marlowe's poetry and uncovered the sexy context of Shakespeare's *Sonnets*. John Boswell's two great books led me to Martial's *Epigrams*, Ovid's *Metamorphoses*, and other bits of classical treasure. Turning full circle, I again examined the story of David and Jonathan in the *Bible*, and found it to be exactly what I had thought it was so long ago: a beautiful love story between two young men. And with my newly informed intelligence, the story of Jesus and John also took on a new and startling color.

My desire is to offer a banquet of illuminating, educating, thought-provoking and challenging selections from both spiritual and philosophical writers in an effort to spare some of today's gay men from the intellectual starvation I experienced when I was young. These writings are both a record of my liberation and a road map for others to follow. It is my hope that this book might speed others along the path that took me too long to travel.

Naturally, this book is <u>not</u> the last word on the subject of gay writing: there are plenty more books where these came from. There are whole civilizations whose writings are unrepresented in this book. I do not for an instant believe that there has ever been a culture in which men have not loved men; but there are plenty of reasons why in many cases we can no longer find any trace of such love. I have done my best with what I have found so far: I look forward to finding [and, if possible, publishing] much more in the future.

This book is primarily concerned with the concept of men loving other men. I have not produced any lengthy arguments in favor of the naturalness and rightness of that love, as I now hold that truth to be self-evident. Other modern gay writers have written long and hard on this subject, and any reader interested can find dozens of such works; Colin Spencer's *Homosexuality in History* is an excellent resource. I also am not terribly concerned here with the mundane facts of the domestic lives of these writers, of who lived with whom, of who was married, and so on. The introductions I have written for each selection are designed to place the writing in the context of other writings in the realm of men loving men. I leave the trivia to their biographers.

I have edited these selections quite freely, and I believe that there has been no gross distortion of the texts as a result. However, space considerations simply did not allow for the inclusion of plenty of good material. I urge my readers to look up the originals of these works and read them. Blake's works, for example, must be viewed in a color copy of the original engravings in order to be appreciated. Shakespeare's *Sonnets* form an organic whole; reading a few poems in isolation gives only a part of the whole story. Oscar Wilde's poems and prose are a splendid gay world all to themselves. All of these books were obtained through public libraries of one sort or another; there are no hidden or secret writings revealed here.

Some who read this book, and many more who don't, will accuse me of Christian bashing. While it might be perfectly fair to claim that "they started it", I think that a bit of historical as well as personal perspective is called for here. First, I must state the truth: hateful homophobes are only the most visible and vocal minority in the churches. The majority of people calling themselves Christians are good and honest people who tolerate, permit and tacitly support hate-mongering when it comes to gays.

Having said that, I have learned that Christian churches have systematically harassed, persecuted, and murdered gay people for many centuries. This persecution peaked during the five hundred year reign of terror called The Inquisition, when accusations of queer sex were as common as witchcraft and heresy, and just as deadly. Also routinely sent to the stake were Jews, Moslems, Wiccans, mid-wives, political dissidents, free-thinkers, and almost anyone else who disagreed with the orthodox church. According to Webster, the term "faggot", meaning a bundle of wood, something to be used as fuel for the fires, dates from the fourteenth century.

Mercifully, our modern state no longer bases execution solely on the authority of Christian churches: we can all breathe a little easier knowing that the Christian Coalition will not be breaking down our doors to drag us to the stakes. But what they can no longer destroy with physical violence, homophobes like Rev. Pat Robertson [leading the fight to destroy the National Endowment for the Arts], Rev. Fred Phelps ["AIDS is God's gift to fags"] and Jesse Helms [who vilified Roberta Achtenberg as a "damned lesbian" on the floor of the United States Senate] attack with hateful lies and wounding words. I grew up listening to extremists like Robertson, and I once debated, via U. S mail, Ben Kinchlow, then co-host of Robertson's TV show, *The 700 Club*. From my own experience I have learned that such modern fundamentalist Christians are intellectual clones of the religious maniacs who burned so many at the stake centuries ago.

I have commented in this work on the on-going Christian persecution of gays for two reasons: first, the history of the Church is inextricably bound up with the history of Western Civilization, and cannot be separated from the fabric of European literature and philosophy; and second, it is a history of persecution with which I am intimately familiar, having lived as a Christian for thirty years before my own liberation.

When I gave the first draft of this work to my friend Herman, he objected (as had my husband) to my original title *A Gay Bible*. After spending a few days with my manuscript, he called and suggested the current title to me, pointing out that the word *testament*, like *testify* and *testimony*, derives from the word *testis*, or testicles. Ironically, the testicles are the primary source of testosterone, the male sex hormone that makes us behave like men. Therefore, *testament* also has the sense of *regarding men*. With this in mind, Herman suggested that *Gay Testaments—Old and New* was the perfect title for this book, and I agreed.

It is my hope that this book will serve as solace and comfort for gay men and for our friends, as a reference and history of our past, and as inspiration for the days to come. These writings have inspired, liberated, and transformed me— and I hope they will do the same for you.

Bela Dornon, San Diego, 1997

PART ONE: PHILOSOPHY

Preceding Page: Chinese characters depicting *Wu Wei,* a core concept in the teachings of Taoism.

Calligraphy: Pascal Gagneux

Lao Tzu
(Approximately 500 BCE)

Western thinking dominates modern America, binding us with an ethic of excess, isolation, conspicuous consumption, and competition. Much of Eastern thought provides an alternative to this unbalanced philosophy; one strand of Eastern thought, Taoism, reached its peak 2,500 years ago with the composition of the *Tao Teh Ching* .

Many colorful traditions surround the birth and life of the man called Lao Tzu, yet little is known for certain about the author of this Chinese philosophical masterpiece. It is believed that the author was a scholar who lived a long life of contemplation and study, fond of obscurity and solitude. Reliable evidence suggests that the master was born in what is now the province of Hunan (then called Ch'u) sometime in the sixth century before the Common Era, where he served as Custodian of the Imperial Archives of the Chou House. According to Henry Wei,

… It was not until the Chou House began to show glaring signs of decay and decline that [Lao Tzu] finally took his departure and decided to exile himself.

As he reached the pass leading westward, the warden of the pass, Yin Hsi, said to him, "Since you are retiring from the world, will you please write a book for my enlightenment?"

Lao Tzu consented and wrote a book in two parts about the meaning of Tao and Teh, consisting of a little over five thousand words....[1]

Since its introduction to Western culture less than two hundred years ago, the *Tao Teh Ching* has gained widespread popularity as an effective series of short poems and essays designed to confuse, illuminate, and immobilize the intellect, finally freezing the restless human consciousness so that the mystery of the universe may unfold before ones eyes.

Although the process of translation from Chinese pictographs into Western phonetic languages has left some of the integral meaning behind, the concepts remaining are richly useful for those interested in meditational discipline, understanding of the human condition, and the path of spiritual evolution.

Internal balance and alignment with Tao is the goal of those who follow the sage's teaching. I believe that we, as gay men, already possess a precious advantage in this pursuit: we are endowed with what the American Indians describe as a double spirit; that is, with easy access to both the masculine and feminine parts of the human personality. It could be said that, as gay men, we are uniquely advantaged in the quest for balance between the masculine and feminine elements. As gay men, we are naturally closer to the ideal of harmony and balance between the male and female. Even in our sexuality, we are able, as straight men cannot, to "play the Female" in the game of love [see poem 28 below]. While no specific mention is made of the sex act in the following passages, the idea of "playing the Female" in bed or in social life is easier for gay men to understand, adopt and appreciate than it is for the majority of straight men.

The following essay, with quotations from Henry Wei's translation, is intended as an introduction to the *Tao Teh Ching* only, and should not under any circumstances be taken as an exhaustive treatment of this wonderfully complex work. Apprehension of the truths contained in the *Tao Teh Ching* comes only through long-term study of the poems themselves.[2]

My own editorial comments appear in brackets.

from *The Guiding Light of Lao Tzu:*

There is something formless and perfect,
Ever-existing, even before birth of Heaven and Earth.
How still it is! How quiet!
Abiding alone and unchanging,
It pervades everywhere without fail.
Well may it be the mother of the world.
I do not know its name,
But label it Tao...[3]

[Namelessness is an essential quality of Tao:]

The Tao that can be stated is not the Eternal Tao.
The name that can be named is not the Eternal Name.
The Unnamable is originator of Heaven and Earth.
The Namable is mother of the ten thousand things....[4]

Without going out of doors,
One can know the world;
Without looking through the window,
One can realize the Way of Heaven.
The farther one goes,
The less one knows.
Therefore, the Sage knows without going out,
Discriminates without seeing,
And accomplishes without action.[5]

[Similarly, human experience of Tao is not limited by
the five senses; in fact, physical and emotional urges merely
hinder perception of and conformity to Tao:]

Therefore,
Always be desireless, so as to discern Tao's wonderful essence;
Always have some desire, so as to discern its manifestations.
These two come out from the same source,
But are different in name....[6]

The five colors blind man's eyes;
The five tones deafen man's ears;
The five flavors vitiate man's taste;
Racing and hunting make man's heart go wild;
Hard-to-get articles impede man's movement....[7]

[Taoist teaching leads to a balance between the yin and
yang elements contained in everything, including the human
soul and body:]

He, who knows the Male,
And yet holds on to the Female,
Becomes the ravine of the world.

Being the ravine of the world,
He is always in union with Eternal Virtue,
And returns to the state of the new-born babe.
He, who knows the white (Yang)
And yet holds on to the black (Yin)
Becomes a model for the world.
Being a model for the world,
His Eternal Virtue becomes unerring,
And he returns to the Infinite....[8]

[Equilibration leads to the attainment of perfection; once perfection is achieved, the soul returns to the Eternal Creative Divinity, which is her origin. The idea here is that masculine energy is thrusting, rising, and intellectual, while feminine energy is emotional, restful, and embracing. A man must reconcile both the masculine and feminine energies within himself to find balance.[9]]

Fine weapons are inauspicious instruments.
They are probably detested by the people.
Therefore, he who is possessed of Tao rejects them....
Weapons are inauspicious instruments;
They are not instruments for the superior man.
He uses them only under dire necessity,
And in this case priority is given to moderation.
He does not consider victory a fine thing.
Those who consider victory a fine thing
Are those who delight in slaughtering people....
Mass slaughter is to be bewailed with grief and sorrow.
Victory is to be mourned with funeral rites.[10]

[Pacifism must be the rule, not the exception, for each individual, city, and state. In order for people to practice non-interference, they must be free from outside oppression, from other people, states, or even governments. Therefore, moderation must be followed in the policies of those who govern the people:]

When the world abounds in prohibitions,

The people will become impoverished.
When men have plenty of weapons in hand,
The state will be in great confusion....
When laws and decrees are numerous and manifest,
Bandits and thieves will increase and multiply....[11]

[One hears quite often today the old saying, "You can't legislate morality." This statement is supported by Taoist ideology, and the reason is simple: right moral behavior results from an inward awareness of Tao, not from legislation aimed at forcing correct behavior out of citizens. In this case, the society and the state can inspire an awareness of Tao through example, but cannot force this awareness through legislation.]

Do not exalt the worthy,
So that the people will not contend.
Do not treasure hard-to-get objects,
So that the people will not become thieves.
Keep what is desirable out of sight,
So that their hearts will not get excited.
Therefore, in ruling the people the sage
Empties their hearts,
Fills their bellies,
Weakens their aspirations,
Strengthens their bones....[12]
Forswear wisdom, discard knowledge,
And the people will gain a thousandfold.
Forswear benevolence, discard righteousness,
And the people will recover filial and parental love.
Forswear skill, discard profit,
And thieves and robbers will not appear.
These three steps are inadequate for culture.
They, therefore, have to encompass some others,
Such as: Display plainness, embrace simplicity,
Reduce selfishness, and decrease desires.[13]

[To the Western mind, accustomed to linear thinking (progress toward a goal; beginning, middle, end), many prescriptions in the Taoist cannon appear ludicrous. This is because western thought has become unbalanced by elevating accomplishment, enshrining competition, and devaluing humility and cooperation. Instead of a linear understanding of life, Taoist theory offers the model of the constant fluctuations of the sine wave:]

Cyclic reversion is Tao's movement.
Weakness is Tao's function.
All things in the Universe are derived from Being.
Being is derived from Non-Being....[14]
Empty the mind to the utmost extent.
Maintain quiescence with the whole being.
The ten thousand things are growing with one impulse,
Yet I can discern their cyclic return.
Luxuriant indeed are the growing things,
Yet each again will return to the root.
Returning to the root means quiescence;
Quiescence means renewal of life;
Renewal of life means in tune with the Immutable.
Knowing the Immutable brings enlightenment.
Not knowing the Immutable brings disaster.
Knowing the Immutable, one will be broad-minded;
Being broad-minded, one will be impartial;
Being impartial, one will be kingly;
Being kingly, one will attain the Divine;
Attaining the Divine, one will merge with Tao,
And become immortal and imperishable,
Even after the disappearance of the body.[15]

[The way to recover individual and social harmony and balance is simple, but profound:]

To learn, one increases day by day;
To cultivate Tao, one reduces day by day.
Reduce and reduce and keep on reducing,
Till the state of non-action is reached.
With non-action there is nothing that cannot be done....[16]
To the good, I show goodness;
To the not good, I also show goodness.

Hence, goodness is realized.
To the sincere, I show sincerity;
To the insincere I also show sincerity;
Hence sincerity is realized....[17]

When the world goes in accord with Tao,
Horses are used for hauling manure.
When the world is out of keeping with Tao,
Horses are reared in the suburbs for war.
No sin is greater than yielding to desires;
No fault greater than hankering after wealth.
Therefore, know contentment!
He who knows contentment is always content.[18]

Hold fast to the Great Form [Tao],
And wherever in the world you go,
You will meet with no harm,
But enjoy security, peace, and well-being....[19]

[Correct priorities are essential to those who would travel The Way:]

Which is more dear: Fame or health?
Which is more valuable: Health or wealth?
Which is more baneful: Gain or loss?
Excessive love is bound to cause great expense.
Immense hoarding is bound to end in heavy loss.
He who knows contentment is free from disgrace....[20]

Favor and disgrace both seem startling.
Honor is great trouble if identified with the self....
The reason why I have great trouble is that I have a self;
If I am selfless and unselfish,
What trouble do I have?...[21]

[Mystic meditation leads to balance:]

In harmonizing your *hun* and *p'o* to embrace the One,
Can you concentrate without deviating?

In attuning your breathing to induce tenderness,
Can you become like a new-born babe?...
When the heavenly Gate opens and closes,
Can you play the part of the Female?...[22]

['Moderation in all things' is a Taoist construction:]

To hold and fill a vessel to brimful
Is not so good as to stop before the limit.
Hone a tool to its sharpest state
And its keenness cannot long be preserved.
A hall filled with gold and jade
Can scarcely be safeguarded.
To show pride in one's wealth and high rank
Is to pave the way for one's own doom.
Retire after achieving success and winning renown!
This is the Way of Heaven....[23]

What is secure can be easily maintained.
What is yet unmanifest can be easily tackled.
What is brittle can easily be broken.
What is puny can easily be scattered.
Act before any trouble starts.
Enforce order before disorder arises.
A big tree, whose girth fills a man's embrace,
Springs from a tender shoot....
A journey of a thousand miles
Begins with a single step....[24]

[The master's description of The Way contains many contra-
dictory riddles, all designed to confuse and stimulate the mind;
intuition, rather than logic, is the key to Tao:]

Practice non-interference.
Assert non-assertion.
Taste the tasteless.
Regard small as great, little as much.
Requite evil with virtue....[25]

He who understands Tao seems confounded by it....[26]

1 The Guiding Light of Lao Tzu: A New Translation and Commentary on the Tao Teh Ching. Henry Wei, Quest Books, 1982, p. 3.

2 In fact, one of the poems (56) begins with a passage which certainly should give any commentator pause: "Those who know do not speak; Those who speak do not know...."

3 Hsiang Yuan (25); compare this to the "Spirit of God" that brooded over the deep in Genesis 1. Translators vary greatly in their treatment of this passage: compare Robert Blackney's translation: "Something there is, whose veiled creation was/ Before the earth or sky began to be;/ So silent, so aloof and so alone,/ It changes not, nor fails, but touches all/ Conceive it as the mother of the world./ I do not know its name;/ A name for it is 'Way' [Tao]..."

4 T'i Tao (1). "Ten thousand things" is a Chinese euphemism for the manifestations of the physical universe, or everything that can be perceived with the five senses.

5 Chien Yuan (47)

6 T'i Tao (1). Wei points out that, "it is correct to say: 'One always feels happy when meeting a good friend, and always feels somewhat sad when saying goodbye to him'." (p. 129) In this sense, the sage's instruction to maintain two seemingly contrary states of mind at the same time is not hard to reconcile.

7 Chien Yu (12)

8 Pan P'u (28)

9 The American society is increasingly unbalanced toward the masculine pole; the elevation and emulation of gay men would easily and painlessly correct this problem, allowing heterosexual males the freedom to experience and share other emotions and behaviors in addition to anger and aggression.

10 Yen Wu (31)

11 Ch'un Feng (57)

12 An Min (3)

13 Huan Ch'un (19)

14 Ch'u Yung (40). Compare Blackney: "The movement of the Way is return;/ In weakness lies its major usefulness./ From What-is all the world of things was born/ But What-is sprang in turn from What-is-not."

15 Kuei Ken (16)

16 Wang Chih (48)

17 Ren Teh (49)

18 Chien Yu (46) R. B. Blackney translates the passage thusly:
"...No sin can exceed/ Incitement to envy;/ No calamity's worse/ Than to be discontented;/ Nor is there an omen/ More dreadful than coveting./ But once be contented,/ And truly you'll always be so."

19 Ren Teh (35)

20 Li Chieh (44)

21 Yen Ch'ih (13)

22 Neng Wei (10)

23 Yun Yi (9)

24 Shou Wei (64)

25 En Shih (63)

26 T'ung I (41)

Plato

(427-347 BCE)

Like Jesus five centuries after him, the philosopher Socrates (469-399 BCE) never wrote a word; his ideas were implanted in the minds of his friends and students and blossomed after his execution in the writings of his students. Plato, Socrates' most famous pupil, shaped his teacher's ideas into long and elegant dialogues, written as if Socrates were speaking to one or more persons in front of an audience. These dialogues became the foundation of classical Greek philosophy, and the basis of Western thought and culture.

In *The Symposium On Love,* Plato creates a partly fictional party at which many prominent Greeks of the time take turns entertaining each other with speeches in praise of gay love. It should be mentioned here that an institutional form of inter-generational gay coupling was promoted among the highest circles in Athens at the time of Plato: an older man would take a younger man as his lover, developing him as a protégé. It is to this form of gay love that the speeches are directed.

The importance of the teachings of Plato and Socrates cannot be overstated: it has been rightly stated that all of Western philosophy since the time of Socrates consists of footnotes to Plato.

from the *Symposium on Love:*

"...I propose that each of us in turn, going from left to right, shall make a speech in honor of Love. Let him give us the best which he can; and Phaedrus, because he is sitting first on the left hand, and because he is the father of the thought, shall begin."...

Phaedrus began by affirming that: "Love is a mighty god.... And...he is also the source of the greatest benefits to us. For I know not any greater blessing to a young man who is beginning life than a virtuous lover, or to the lover than a beloved youth. For the principle which ought to be the guide of men who would nobly live—that principle, I say, neither kindred, nor honor, nor wealth, nor any other motive is able to implant so well as love. Of what am I speaking? Of the sense of honor and dishonor, without which neither states nor individuals ever do any good or great work. And I say that a lover who is detected in doing any dishonorable act…will be more pained at being detected by his beloved than at being seen by his father, or his companions, or by anyone else. The beloved, too, when he is found in any disgraceful situation, has the same feeling about his lover. And if there were only some way of contriving that a state or army should be made up of lovers and their loves, they would be the very best governors of their own city, abstaining from all dishonor, and emulating one another in honor; and when fighting at each other's sides, though a mere handful, they would overcome the world…. Love will make men dare to die for their beloved —love alone…

"[Think of] the true love of Akhilleus toward his lover Patróklos — his lover, and not his love (the notion that Patróklos was the beloved one is a foolish notion into which Aeschylus has fallen, for Akhilleus was surely the fairer of the two, also than all the other heroes; and, as Homer informs us, he was still beardless and younger far). And greatly as the gods honor the virtue of love, still the return of love on the part of the beloved to the lover is more admired and valued by them, for the lover is more divine, because he is inspired by God. Now Akhilleus was quite aware, for he had been told by his mother, that he might avoid death and return home and live to a good old age, if he abstained from slaying Hector. None the less he gave his life to avenge his friend, and dared to die, not only in his defense, but after he was dead.[1] Wherefore the gods honored him [highly] and sent him to the Isle of the Blest. These are my reasons for affirming that Love is the eldest and noblest and mightiest of the gods, and the chiefest author and giver of virtue in life, and of happiness after death."

This, or something like it, was the speech of Phaedrus; and some other speeches followed which Aristomedus did not remember; the next which he repeated was that of Pausanias, [who explains that there are two goddesses of Love; one ancient and immortal, and the other born recently and in the normal way.]

"...Those who are inspired by [the nobler goddess of love] turn to the male, and delight in him who is the more valiant and intelligent nature; anyone may recognize the pure enthusiasts in the very character of their attachments. For they love not boys, but intelligent beings whose reason is beginning to be developed, much about the time that their beards begin to grow. And in choosing young men to be their companions, they mean to be faithful to them, and pass their whole life in company with them, not to take them in their inexperience and deceive them, and play the fool with them, or run away from one to another of them. But the love of young boys should be forbidden by law, because their future is uncertain; they may turn out good or bad, either in body or soul, and much noble enthusiasm may be thrown away upon them; in this matter the good are a law to themselves, and the coarser[2] sort of lovers ought to be restrained by force, as we restrain or attempt to restrain them from fixing their affections on freeborn women. These are the people who bring a reproach on love; and some have been led to deny the lawfulness of such attachments, because they see the impropriety and evil of them....

"The rules about love are perplexing... the law is simply in favor of these connections, and no one, young or old, has anything to say to their discredit... In countries which are subject to the barbarians, the custom [of men loving youths] is held to be dishonorable; lovers of youths share the evil repute in which gymnastics and philosophy are held, because they are inimical to tyranny; for the interests of rulers require that their subjects should be poor in spirit, and that there should be no strong bond of friendship or society among them, which love, above all other motives, is likely to inspire, as our Athenian tyrants learned by examples; for the love of Aristogeiton and the constancy of Harmodius[3] had a strength which undid their power....

"The actions of a lover have a grace which ennobles them... From this point of view a man fairly argues that in Athens to love and be loved is held to be fairly honorable...such practices are honorable to him who follows them honorably, dishonorable to him who follows them dishonorably.... [A] hasty attachment is held to be dishonorable, because time is the true test of this as of most other things; and secondly there is a dishonor in being overcome by the love of money, or of wealth, or of political power, whether a man is frightened into surrendering by the loss of them, or, having experienced the benefits of money and political corruption, is unable to rise above the seductions of them. For none of these things are of a permanent or lasting nature; not to mention that no generous friendship ever sprang from them...."

...Aristophanes professed to open another vein of discourse; he had a mind to praise Love in another way, unlike that of either Pausanias or Eryximachus.

"Mankind," he said, "judging by their neglect of him, have never, as I think, at all understood the power of Love. For if they had understood him they would surely have built noble temples and altars, and offered solemn sacrifice in his honor; but that is not done, and most certainly ought to be done: since of all the gods he is the best friend of men, the helper and healer of the ills which are the great impediment to the happiness of the race. I will try to describe his power to you, and you shall teach the rest of the world what I am teaching you.

"In the first place, let me treat of the nature of man, and of what has happened to it; for the original human nature was not like the present, but different. The sexes were not two as they are now, but three in number; there was man, woman, and the union of the two, having [the] name "androgynous"...because the sun, moon and earth are three; and the man was originally a child of the sun, the woman of the earth, and the man-woman of the moon, which is made up of sun and earth.... Terrible was their might and strength... and they made an attack upon the gods...

"Zeus said, 'Methinks I have a plan which will humble their pride and improve their manners; men shall continue to exist, but I will cut them in two and they will be diminished in strength and increased in numbers; this will have the advantage of making them more profitable to us. They shall walk upright on two legs...'

"He spoke and cut men in two... Apollo was also bidden to heal their wounds and compose their forms....After the[ir] division the two parts of man, each desiring his other half, came together, and throwing their arms about one another, entwined in mutual embraces, longing to grow into one…

"Zeus in pity of them invented a new plan: he turned the organs of generation round to the front… the male generated in the female in order that by the mutual embraces of man and woman they might breed, and the race might continue; or if man came to man they might be satisfied, and rest, and go their ways to the business of life: so ancient is the desire for one another which is implanted in us, reuniting our original nature, making one of two, and healing the state of man.

"Each of us when separated, having one side only, like a flat fish, is but the indenture of a man, and he is always looking for his other half. Men who are a section of that double nature which was once called androgynous are lovers of women…the women who are sections of a woman do not care for men, but have female attachments; the female companions are of this sort. But they who are a section of the male follow the male, and while they are young, being slices of the original male, they hang about men and embrace them, and they are themselves the best of boys and youths, because they have the most manly nature. Some indeed assert that they are shameless, but this is not true; for they do not act thus from any want of shame, but because they are valiant and manly, and have a manly countenance, and they embrace that which is like them…. When they reach manhood they are lovers of youth, and are not naturally inclined to marry or beget children—if at all they do so only in obedience to the law; but they are satisfied if they may be allowed to live with one another unwedded; and such a nature is prone to love and ready to return love, always embracing that which is akin to him. And when one of them meets with his other half, the actual half of himself, whether he be a lover of youth or a lover of another sort, the pair are lost in an amazement of love and friendship and intimacy, and one will not be out of the other's sight, as I may say, even for a moment: these are the people who pass their whole lives together; yet they could not explain what they desire of one another.

"Suppose Hephaestus,[4] with his instruments, were to come upon the pair that are lying side by side and say to them, 'What do you people want of one another?' they would be unable to answer. And suppose further, that when he saw their perplexity he said, 'Do you desire to be wholly one; always day and night to be in one another's company? For if this is your desire, I am ready to melt you into one and let you grow together, so being two you may become one, and while you live a common life as if you were a single man, and after your death in the world below still be one departed soul instead of two; I ask whether this is what you lovingly desire, and whether you are satisfied to attain this?'—there is not a man of them who, when he heard the proposal, would deny or would not acknowledge that this meeting and melting into one another, this becoming one instead of two, was the very expression of his ancient need.

"And the reason is that human nature was originally one and we were a whole, and the desire and pursuit of the whole is called love.... Love is to us the lord and minister; and let no one oppose him—he is the enemy of the gods who opposes him. For if we are friends of the god and at peace with him, we shall find our own true loves, which rarely happens in this world at present. I am serious, and therefore I must beg Eryximachus not to make fun or find any allusion in what I am saying to Pausanias and Agathon, who, as I suspect, are both of the manly nature, and belong to the class which I have been describing. But my words have a wider application—they include men and women everywhere; and I believe that if our loves were perfectly accomplished, and each of us returning to his primal nature had his original true love, then our race would be happy. And if this would be best of all, the best in the next degree and under present circumstances must be the nearest approach to such a union; and that will be the attainment of a genial love...."

"...Very good..." said Agathon. "I see no reason why I should not proceed with my speech....Love...is the tenderest as well as the youngest [god]...All men in all things serve him of their own free will, and where there is voluntary agreement, there, as the laws which are the lords of the city say, is justice.... Love set in order the empire of the gods....[Love] is the friend of the good, the wonder of the wise, the amazement of the gods; desired by those who have no part in him, and precious to those who have the better part in him… in every word, work, wish, fear—savior, pilot, comrade, helper; glory of gods and men, leader best and brightest; in whose footsteps let every man follow, sweetly singing in his honor and joining in that sweet strain with which love charms the souls of gods and men…"

When Agathon had done speaking, Aristomedus said that there was a general cheer; the young man was thought to have spoken in a manner worthy of himself.

"Why, my dear friend," said Socrates, "…I am especially struck by the beauty of the concluding words—who could listen to them without amazement?…

"But if you like to hear to the truth about love, I am ready to speak in my own manner…. I will rehearse a tale of love which I heard from Diotima of Mantinea, a woman wise in this and many other kinds of knowledge…. She was my instructor in the art of love, and I shall repeat to you what she said to me….

"'Think,' she said, '…of the ambition of men, and you will wonder at the senselessness of their ways, unless you consider how they are stirred by the love of an immortality of fame. They are ready to run all risks greater far than they would have run for their children, and to spend money and undergo any sort of toil, and even to die, for the sake of leaving behind them a name which shall be eternal….

"'Those who are pregnant in the body only betake themselves to women and beget children—this is the character of their love; their offspring, as they hope, will preserve their memory and give them the blessedness and immortality which they desire in the future. But *souls* which are pregnant—for there certainly are men who are more creative in their souls than in their bodies—conceive that which is proper for the soul to conceive or contain. And what are these conceptions?—wisdom and virtue in general. And such creators are poets and all artists who are deserving of the name inventor.

"'But the greatest and fairest sort of wisdom by far is the sort that is concerned with ordering of states and families, and which is called temperance and justice. And he who in youth has the seed of these implanted and is himself inspired, when he comes to maturity desires to beget and generate. He wanders about seeking beauty that he may beget offspring—for in deformity he will beget nothing—and naturally embraces the beautiful rather than the deformed body; above all, when he finds a fair and noble and well-nurtured soul, he embraces the two in one person, and to such a one he is full of speech about the virtue and the nature and the pursuit of a good man; and he tries to educate him; and at the touch of the beautiful which is ever present to his memory, even when absent, he brings forth that which he had conceived long before, and in company with him tends that which he brings forth; and they are married by a far nearer tie and have a closer friendship than those who beget mortal children, for the children who are their common offspring are fairer and more immortal. Who, when he thinks of Homer and Hesiod and other great poets, would not rather have their children[5] than ordinary human ones? Who would not emulate them in the creation of children such as theirs, which have preserved their memory and given them everlasting glory?… And many temples have been raised in their honor for the sake of children such as theirs; which were never raised in honor of anyone, for the sake of his mortal children.

"'These are the lesser mysteries of love, into which even you, Socrates, may enter; to the greater and more hidden ones which are the crown of these, and to which you, if you pursue them in a right spirit, they will lead, I know not whether you will be able to attain. But I will do my utmost to inform you, and do you follow if you can. For he who would proceed aright in these matters should begin in youth to visit beautiful forms; and first, if he be guided by his instructor aright, to love one such form only—out of that he should create fair thoughts; and soon he will of himself perceive that the beauty of one form is akin to the beauty of another; and then if beauty of form in general is his pursuit, how foolish would he be not to recognize that the beauty in every form is one and the same! And when he perceives this he will abate his violent love of the one, which he will despise and deem a small thing, and will become a lover of all beautiful forms; in the next stage he will consider that the beauty of the mind is more honorable than the beauty of the outward form. So that if a virtuous soul have but a little comeliness, he will be content to love and tend him, and will search out and bring to the birth thoughts which may improve the young, until he is compelled to contemplate and see the beauty of institutions and laws, and to understand that the beauty of them all is of one family, and that personal beauty is a trifle; and after laws and institutions he will go on to the sciences, that he may see their beauty, being not like a servant in love with the beauty of one youth or man or institution, himself a slave and narrow-minded, but drawing toward and contemplating the vast sea of beauty, he will create many fair and noble thoughts and notions in boundless love of wisdom; until on that shore he waxes and grows strong, and at last the vision is revealed to him of a single science, which is the science of beauty everywhere....[T]he true order of going, or being led by another, to the things of love, is to begin from the beauties of the earth and mount upwards for the sake of the other beauty, using these as steps only, and from one going to two, and from two going to all fair forms, and from fair forms to fair practices, and from fair practices to fair notions, until from fair notions he arrives at the notion of absolute beauty, and at last knows what the essence of beauty is. This, my dear Socrates,' said the stranger of Mantinea, 'is that life above all others which man should live, in the contemplation of beauty absolute; a beauty which if you once beheld, you would see not to be after the measure of gold, and garments, and fair boys and youths, whose presence now entrances you; and you and many a one would be content to live seeing them only and conversing with them without meat or drink, if that were possible—you only want to look at them and be with them. But what if man had eyes to see true beauty—the divine beauty, I mean, pure and clear and unalloyed, not clogged with the pollutions of mortality and all the colors and vanities of human life—thither looking, and holding converse with the true beauty simple and divine? Remember how in that communion only, beholding beauty with the eye of the mind, he will be enabled to bring forth, not images of beauty, but realities (for he has hold not of an image but of a reality), and bringing forth and nourishing true virtue to become the friend of God and immortal, if mortal man may? Would that be an ignoble life?'

"Such... were the words of Diotima; and I am persuaded of their truth....[T]hat in the attainment of this end human nature will not easily find a better helper than love. And therefore, also, I will say that every man ought to honor him as I honor him, and walk in his ways, and exhort others to do the same, and praise the power and spirit of love according to the measure of my ability now and ever...."

When Socrates had done speaking, the company applauded, and Aristophanes was beginning to say something in answer to the allusions that Socrates had made to his own speech, when suddenly there was a great knocking at the door of the house, as of revelers, and the sound of a flute-girl was heard....

[concluded in PART TWO: LITERATURE]

1 Compare this to Homer's account, and to Wilde's summary of Homer and of Plato.

2 Plato refers here to men of a lower social class.

3 Attic lovers who, at the cost of their own lives, started the revolt that overthrew the tyranny of the sons of Piesistratus in 510 BCE, opening the way for democracy.

4 The Greek god of fire and metallurgy, whom the Romans named Vulcan.

5 The Iliad, The Odyssey, and other great classics of Greek literature.

Marianne Williamson

In Plato's *Symposium on Love,* Socrates claims that he was instructed in the philosophy of love by Diotima, a mysterious wise woman from Mantinea. Today we are all fortunate to enjoy the same level of spiritual guidance from Marianne Williamson, a modern instructor in the ancient philosophy of love.

Ms. Williamson gained success and popularity in the early 1990s with her accessible commentaries on *A Course In Miracles.* In her introduction to *A Return To Love*, Williamson offers a contemporary restatement of what Christopher Isherwood called "The Perennial Philosophy". It is a declaration of hope and inclusion for all people, in all circumstances.

from *A Return To Love:*

When we were born, we were programmed perfectly. We had a natural tendency to focus on love. Our imaginations were creative and flourishing, and we knew how to use them. We were connected to a world much richer than the one we connect to now, a world full of enchantment and a sense of the miraculous....

We were taught to think unnaturally. We were taught a very bad philosophy, a way of looking at the world that contradicts who we are.

We were taught to think thoughts like competition, struggle, sickness, finite resources, limitation, guilt, bad, death, scarcity, and loss. We began to think these things were real. We were taught that things like grades, being good enough, money, and doing things right are more important than love. We were taught that we are separate from other people, that we have to compete to get ahead, that we're not quite good enough the way we are. We were taught to see the world the way that others had come to see it. It's as though, as soon as we got here, we were given a sleeping pill. The thinking of the world, which is not based on love, began pounding in our ears the minute we hit shore.

Love is what we were born with. Fear is what we have

learned here. The spiritual journey is the relinquishment—or unlearning—of fear and the acceptance of love back into our hearts. Love is the essential existential fact. It is our ultimate reality and our purpose on earth. To be consciously aware of it, to experience love in ourselves and others, is the meaning of life....

Life spent with any other purpose in mind is meaningless, contrary to our nature, and ultimately painful. It's as though we've been lost in a dark, parallel universe where things are loved more than people. We overvalue what we perceive with our physical senses, and undervalue what we know to be true in our hearts....

Love is the intuitive knowledge of our hearts. It's a 'world beyond' that we all secretly long for. An ancient memory of this love haunts all of us all the time, and beckons us to return.

Love isn't material. It's energy. It's the feeling in a room, a situation, a person....We experience it as kindness, giving, compassion, peace, joy, acceptance, non-judgment, joining, and intimacy.

Fear is our shared lovelessness, our individual and collective hells. It's a world that seems to press on us from within and without, giving constant false testimony to the meaninglessness of love. When fear is expressed, we recognize it as anger, abuse, disease, pain, greed, addiction, selfishness, obsession, corruption, violence and war.

Love is within us. It cannot be destroyed, but can only be hidden. The world we knew as children is still buried within our minds....

And that's what a miracle is: a parting of the mists, a shift in perception, a return to love.

"Michael"

Chelsea Quinn Yarbro's *Messages From Michael* modernizes and expands the ancient oracular tradition of acquiring wisdom through mediums and/or physical objects. The ancient Hebrews used the technique with their ephod, Urim and Thummim, the mechanical objects through which their god, Yahweh, communicated with the temple priests. Many ancient cultures used objects such as embers, internal organs, and even animal droppings to divine the future. Special mediums or messengers, individuals believed able to "tune in" to the Divine, would interpret signs, deliver messages from the gods, and proclaim the destiny of humans on request. Roman Catholics use an elected Pope for this purpose, believing that he alone can reveal infallible teachings from God. The Mormon church was founded by Joseph Smith allegedly using magical glasses to decode ancient writings on golden tablets.

In Yarbro's *Messages,* information arrives via Ouija board in answer to questions posed by a small band of occult adventurers.[1] According to Yarbro, only the names of the group members were changed; the source of the wisdom in this case is an entity known as "Michael", who identify themselves[2] as humans who have completed their series of incarnations on Earth, and who have returned on a mission: to disseminate to mankind a new system for understanding ourselves and the human condition.

The arrangement, section headings, and editing of the following selections are my own. Numbers in parentheses indicate page numbers. My own editorial comments appear in brackets.

from *Messages From Michael*:

Introduction

…This teaching is offered to you freely and without conditions.… We do not promise a paradise, or, for that matter, a hell, either, only progressive evolution, the ultimate state of which is bliss, and which you will achieve with or without our help…To our knowledge there is no teaching now extant on the physical plane with access to the universal truths that many of you credit them with.…This system is offered with love. Belief or faith is definitely not required, or even desired, for evolution will happen to you whether or not you believe.…(281-284)   Belief is not required; you will reincarnate anyway. A leaf does not have to believe in photosynthesis to turn green.…(27)

…[We wish] to teach some understanding of the evolution on the physical plane so that [individuals] can reach some insight into human behavior which will enable [them] to then stop brooding over interpersonal relationships or the lack thereof and concentrate on personal life plans…(21)

The human condition

You are part of something much greater than you know, and most of you fear to realize this.…(36)

There is no exalted purpose behind human life. The life itself is the purpose and is only one stage of evolution, which proceeds in an awesomely ordered, unalterable line until the created in effect evolves to become the creator.…(22)

All souls, or fragments, as we choose to call them at this time, are… part of the universal creative force, which we call the Tao. However, when this fragmentation occurs and the physical cycle begins, this fragment is more remote from the Tao and from what we call the Infinite Soul.…(63)

Each soul is part of a larger body, an entity. Each entity consists of about one thousand souls, each of which enters the physical plane as many times as necessary to experience all aspects of human life and achieve human understanding. At the end of the cycles on the physical plane, the fragments once again reunite.…(20)

Entire entities are cast from the Tao. They fragment into physically trapped souls for as long as is necessary for them to experience all of life through the cycles… The continuous creative force that is universal casts out entities into physical lifetimes. These entities fragment and become many different personalities. Their integration is the evolutionary pattern for all souls. You do not feel the desire to seek the remaining fragments of your entity until the last physical cycle. Then, at that time, there is almost a compulsion, you do not know always why you do, but you always seek....(65)

Let us use an analogy and perhaps this will become crystal clear. Imagine the Atlantic ocean as the whole; imagine filling ten test tubes, then sealing them so that they are airtight and watertight, then imagine dropping them back into the ocean. They are a part of the whole, yes, but unless some outside force liberates them, they are remote from the source and trapped in an effective prison. This same way the soul is trapped in the body. The body is very limited in what it can do. The soul in its true spiritual state has no limitations or handicaps....(64)

Human understanding is the lesson of the physical plane; without it, there can be no growth of the soul. To strive for spiritual enlightenment without gaining human understanding is to disregard the real purpose of your existence on the physical plane....(24)

...Humans invariably reincarnate in human form...(270)

When souls are first cast into a dominant species, some, or rather many, of the instinctive drives of the creature of no reason still remain embedded with the biocomputer...before souls were cast, the creatures of no reason from which you have ascended were largely governed by fear, and their lives were taken up in many ceaseless battles for survival.... The battle for survival is but another tape loop that plays on and on, even to the point of starving large portions of the culture, while others waste and hoard....(61)

The 'human' soul, or essence...is a separate entity from the personality, which is for the most part a survival mechanism for the body. The soul's goal is distinct from those of the personality and therefore the elements are in eternal conflict. This is the lesson learned on the physical plane. Only the soul can ask, "why am I here?" The personality does not require such information....(65)

...We remind you that between lives the soul is capable of total review.... You, as you are now, are a script that you yourself have written for your earthbound soul to play. It is perpetual....(169)

...As growth progresses, the soul seeks simplicity....(174)

All ensouled species or conscious creatures of the physical plane have the same roles in essence:[3] slave, artisan, warrior, scholar, sage, priest, and king....all have the same centers from which to act: intellectual, emotional, sexual, instinctive, moving, higher emotional and higher intellectual....(268-269)

...The climb to each new experience is chosen for the particular lifetime and is marked by resting places... then all of a sudden the soul is galvanized into action. This always heralds the approach of a major monad in a soul's life and is many times marked by a change that can be seen by friends... the first is birth, when the body is ensouled. The behavior *in utero* is a function of body type.... The second monad—or, if you prefer to think of it another way, we will call it a milestone—occurs when the fragment realizes that it is surrounded by others who are distinct and different from itself and that those others can influence it emotionally and intellectually as well as instinctively. This milestone usually occurs about age two....

The third milestone occurs at the onset of young adulthood when the fragment is out of "the nest". All of childhood occurs between the second and the third milestone.

The fourth milestone is the so-called mid-life crisis that occurs around age thirty-five at the manifestation of the essence.

The fifth milestone occurs in life when the fragment is a "senior citizen", and has to do in part with the reconciliation of the aspirations with the accomplishments of the particular life.

The sixth occurs at the time of the onset of the final physical deterioration and is concerned with the dynamics of the dying process itself.

The seventh is, of course, the exit itself.

It should be noted here that if this process is intercepted during a lifetime, for instance by violent or early death from illness, the fragment rarely advances a level. A fragment can usually advance through a level of experience only by going through the entire process....(217-218)

Spirituality

The Infinite Soul perceives the Tao....The Infinite Soul has direct access to all knowledge and has no need for education of any kind....the religion of the Infinite Soul is the Logos....(79)

The Infinite Soul manifested through the physical forms of Lao-Tzu, Sri Krishna, Siddhartha Guatama, and Jesus—no others. (85)

...Greek thought had much influence on the man Jesus, particularly Epicurus...Epicurus had a most profound influence on all the philosophy of the time, surpassing that of the stoic Zeno....Jesus was not against sex. He was for moderation. Prostitution is not moderate, even temple prostitution....the man you call Jesus[4] did not die on the cross but died later....he was married...

Honesty without guile, simplicity without poverty of the soul, emptying the life of all non-essential considerations, the endless cycles of evolution with the physical plane being the cruelest and roughest: these are the things emphasized in the true teachings of Christ...(176-180)

Today's Christianity bears little resemblance to the teachings of the man Jesus or to the Logos brought to bear by the Infinite Soul.... Much of the chronology of the events in this man's life is confused, distorted, and in some instances wholly fictionalized....(183)

The beginning of Taoism occurred at the time of the manifestation of the Infinite Soul through Lao Tzu, which you may regard as a title rather than a name. Taoism in its present form is the most undiluted example of the Logos extant. Because of its simplicity, it is often difficult to understand, as most students prefer complexity and complications to this simplicity....[Taoism remains undiluted] because of a lack of foreign intrusion. Also, we would say that since most students find the simplicity baffling, there has been little embellishment. You must remember that Taoism is for the most part free from personification and therefore offers the student an uncluttered view of the Logos....(187)

Sexuality

...We do not recommend rigid structured male-female relationships where there is no room for blooming or growing...There is a weird sort of estrus operating in all humans that makes them seek out a sexual partner. The societal mores demand that they cement this into a more binding contract....sexual expression of love is as valid and beneficial as any other, but because of social pressures and expectations it is more subject to maya[5] than almost any other aspect of human life....(202-203)

...We must emphasize that all aspects of sexuality will be experienced during the cycles, those sexual relationships approved by your society and those that are not....all of you will have homosexual lives. However, you do not specifically choose to be homosexual or heterosexual before rebirth but you do to some extent set up the circumstances that lead to this choice. The choice to be homosexual or heterosexual is made very early in life, usually before the third year—your psychoanalysts are right about that. This choice is usually final and irrevocable and later attempts to alter it either way are very rarely successful. In your culture there are other factors influencing these choices, which are made so early in childhood that the personality is ill-equipped to make them. On the fringe of this are the true bisexual or ambisexual people who are without exception older souls who have lost their strong sense of gender identity and have freed themselves to love whoever comes along in whatever way seems most appropriate at the present moment. Remember that even Jesus said we should love one another....(204)

...The soul is not of the physical plane. How could it possibly have a gender and what good would it be? There is no gender to an entity, and the fragments of an entity have no gender. Male and female are factors of the physical plane....(84)

...There are no sexed souls. (88)

...Those who insist that gender differences have any validity beyond the body do not understand the nature of the higher planes...(223)

Miscellaneous

...Ritual is an enjoyable game which fragments play on the physical plane and we see no harm in that, as such. It is as good a way as any to promote a group high, but it is not good for much else....(180)

Unfulfilled expectations are the sole cause of anger.... When you stop expecting, there will be no anger....(195)

There are two [ensouled] species on this planet, human beings and cetaceans. That is, whales and dolphins. However, we think that you should know that there are over ten million ensouled species in this galaxy alone....(268)

[In regards to efforts to communicate with cetaceans,] You cannot communicate with your fellow humans. Why should you extend the confusion beyond your species? However, we will say this: the cetaceans have evolved so that they have hearing as their dominant sense, as you have sight. You relate to the world visually and they relate to it aurally. If you wish them to understand you, we would suggest that music, the more melodious and complex the better, would be much appreciated by these fragments....(269)

...[Regarding] UFO's...most are simply what their name implies—unidentified flying objects. A few are robot monitors. A few are making studies. A few are lost. A few are what you would probably call tourists. They do not all represent one species. They are from many places and cultures....(270)

1 The Ouija board is an instrument about two feet square with letters and numbers on it; over the board, a planchette with a pointer is moved by one or more people who place their finger tips on the planchette and guide it across the board to spell out words.

2 An entity is defined as a thousand or more souls which, having completed their evolution here on earth, have reunited on the causal plane and are preparing to evolve to the next level of being.

3 *Essence* here refers to the vital substance of the soul itself, its immortal component, its spark of divinity, which comes in seven different types.

4 *Jesus* is the Latin word for the Hebrew name Yeshuaë

5 *Maya* is a term for anything which distracts one from meditation and spiritual awareness.

William Blake

(1757-1827)

For centuries, the Christian church violently suppressed all efforts to translate the Bible into common European languages: until the mid sixteenth century, translators who defied the church's authority were burned as heretics. To a lesser extent, the church also regulated and carefully controlled literacy, in an effort to minimize heresy. But even as the "Age of Reason" gave way to the Industrial Revolution, a similar revolution of ideas and social dynamics was transforming Europe. The Christian church and the individual states each began to diminish in power; individuals and corporations began to assume a larger role in the social order; and as literacy and scriptural translations spread, the church's tight control of art and literature began to decay.

Trained in youth as an artist, William Blake made his living as a painter until his work became too extreme for commercial success; he lived the last half of his life in obscurity and died at seventy, having surrounded himself with a small group of disciples towards the end of his life. His marriage appears to have brought him little joy, and he poured the majority of his energies into his creative works. For Blake, poetry, prose and painting eventually fused into one art form, in which he would paint texts and pictures together, much in the form of modern graphic novels.

Blake's writings proclaim the triumph of reason and experience over blind faith and obedience, and a return to wholeness through full participation in the realm of human sensuality. His insistence on the necessity of broad human experience as a mode of growth brought him condemnation from the church, and isolation from his peers.

In his explosively heretical multi-media presentation *The Marriage of Heaven and Hell,* Blake challenged accepted church doctrines regarding everything from good and evil to the idea that sexuality was a degraded and sinful aspect of humanity. By denying the church's right to demonize human sexuality, Blake paved the way for the next wave of European libertines, whose work in turn inspired the beginnings of the modern gay liberation movement.

Since Blake's *Marriage of Heaven and Hell* is created in a graphic arts format, the irregularities in his spelling and grammar are considered integral to the work, and I have retained them.

from *Songs of Experience:*

The Garden of Love

I went to the Garden of Love,
And saw what I had never seen:
A Chapel was built in the midst,
Where I used to play on the green.

And the gates of this Chapel were shut,
And "Thou Shalt Not" writ over the door;
So I turn'd to the Garden of Love,
That so many sweet flowers bore,

And I saw it was filled with graves,
And tomb-stones where flowers should be:
And Priests in black gowns were walking their rounds,
And binding with briars my joys & desires.

(1794)

from *The Marriage of Heaven and Hell:*

The voice of the Devil

All Bibles or sacred codes have been the causes of the following Errors:
1. That Man has two real existing principles: Viz: a Body & a Soul.
2. That Energy, calld Evil, is alone from the Body, & that Reason, calld Good, is alone from the Soul.

3. That God will torment Man in Eternity for following his energies. But the following Contraries to these are true:

1. Man has no Body distinct from his soul; for that calld Body is a portion of Soul discerned by the five senses, the chief inlets of Soul in this age.

2. Energy is the only life, and is from the Body; and Reason is the bound or outward circumference of Energy.

3. Energy is eternal delight.

Proverbs of Hell:

Prisons are built with stones of Law, Brothels with bricks of religion....
The bird a nest, the spider a web, man friendship....
What is now prov'd was once only imagined....
The soul of sweet delight can never be defil'd....
As the plow follows words, so God follows prayers....
As the caterpillar chooses the fairest leaf to lay her eggs on, so the priest lays his curse on the fairest joys....
Exuberance is beauty....
Sooner murder an infant in its cradle than nurse unacted desires....

A Memorable Fancy:

The ancient Poets animated all things with Gods or Geniuses, calling them by the names and adorning them with the properties of woods, rivers, mountains, lakes, cities, nations, and whatever their enlarged and numerous senses could perceive.

And particularly they studied the genius of each city & country, placing it under its mental deity.

Till a system was formed which some took advantage of & enslav'd the vulgar by attempting to realize or abstract the mental deities from their objects; thus began Priesthood,

Choosing forms of worship from poetic tales,

And at length they announced that the Gods had ordered such things.

Thus men forgot that All deities reside in the human breast.

...Opposition is true Friendship.

Jesus and John

Controversy surrounds the historical accuracy of the Greek writings called the Gospels; formed in some cases more than a century after the events described, and composed of bits and pieces of oral histories, the writings may contain many inaccuracies and mistakes. Though commonly used to condemn gay men, some of these ancient writings portray same-sex relationships in a favorable light. Remembering that sexual orientation is different than behavior, several key points should be kept in mind:

◊　　　John, the presumed author of the Gospel which bears his name, consistently refers to himself as "the beloved disciple" or as "the disciple whom Jesus loved", which, in the Greek literature of his time, was a specific term referring to the younger half of a male-male relationship. (Boswell documents at some length the history of this article of faith within the Christian church.)

◊　　　The Gospels make no mention of any marriage regarding Jesus; Christian doctrine asserts that Jesus had no wife.[1]

◊　　　No recorded words attributed to Jesus say anything, positive or negative, about gay men, although the Gospels record many of His words regarding Love.

from *The Revised Standard Version of the Bible*

...Now before the feast of the Passover, when Jesus knew that his hour had come to depart out of this world to the Father, having loved his own who were with him in the world, he loved them to the end....

Jesus...rose from supper, laid aside his garments, and girded himself with a towel. Then he poured water into a basin, and began to wash the disciples' feet, and to wipe them with the towel with which he was girded....

When he had washed their feet, and taken his garments, and resumed his place, he said to them, "Do you know what I have done to you? You call me Teacher and Lord; and you are right, for so I am. If I then, your Lord and Teacher, have washed your feet, you also ought to wash one another's feet....

"Truly, truly, I say to you, one of you will betray me."...

One of the disciples, whom Jesus loved,[2] was lying close to the breast of Jesus;[3] so Simon Peter beckoned to him and said, "Tell us who it is of whom he speaks."

So lying thus, close to the breast of Jesus, he said to him, "Lord, who is it?"

Jesus answered, "It is he to whom I shall give this morsel after I have dipped it....

"A new commandment I give to you, that you love one another. By this all men will know that you are my disciples, if you have love for one another....This is my commandment, that you love one another as I have loved you. Greater love has no man than that he lay down his life for his friends....This I command you, to love one another...."

So the band of soldiers and their captain and the officers of the Jews seized Jesus and bound him...[4]

And a young man followed him, with nothing but a linen cloth about his body; and they seized him, but he left the linen cloth and ran away naked.[5]

Simon Peter followed Jesus, and so did another disciple. As this disciple was known to the high priest, he entered the court of the high priest along with Jesus, while Peter stood outside at the door....

So they took Jesus and...they crucified him....

But standing by the cross of Jesus were his mother, and his mother's sister, Mary the wife of Clopas, and Mary Magdalene. When Jesus saw his mother, and the beloved disciple standing near, he said to his mother, "Woman, behold your son!" Then he said to the disciple, "Behold, your mother!" And from that hour the disciple took her to his own home....

...the disciple whom Jesus loved, who had lain close to his breast at the supper...This is the disciple who is bearing witness to these things, and who has written these things; and he knows that his witness is true....[6]

"...He who does not love abides in death...

"...Beloved, if our hearts do not condemn us, we have confidence before God...

"...Beloved, let us love one another; for love is of God, and he who loves is born of God and knows God....Beloved, if God so loved us, we also ought to love one another. No man has ever seen God; if we love one another, God abides in us and his love is perfected in us....

"...There is no fear in love, but perfect love casts out fear. For fear has to do with punishment, and he who fears is not perfected in love...." [7]

1 Since the Dark Ages, the church has used this "fact" as the reason why Catholic priests may not marry women. Other teachings contradict the modern church's assertion that Jesus had no wife, among them the teaching of Michael; see above. The customs of Jesus' time seem to have required marriage; it would have been quite remarkable had Jesus never married.

2 In many versions, the term "beloved" is used, which is the usual term for the younger, passive partner in a gay couple.

3 Despite the impression of Leonardo da Vinci's famous fresco, textual evidence indicates that the Last Supper was eaten reclining at table, in the style of the Greeks. See Symposium note, above. For additional information, see Boswell, "Same Sex Marriages..."

4 John 13-18

5 Mark 14

6 John 18-21

7 1 John 3-4

Satguru Sivaya Subramuniyaswami

In his 1993 introduction to the massive Hindu catechism *Dancing with Siva*, Satguru Sivaya Subramuniyaswami describes the monumental volume on Hindu religious tradition as a book that "contains a new presentation of very ancient knowledge." The mystic principles which the reader encounters in the book are not revelations of a strange truth, according to Subramuniyaswami, but rather a restatement of what is already deeply known. Similarly, the practical social wisdom found in the catechism is based on common sense, rather than divine revelation.

Hindu teaching places great reliance on tradition, on intuition, and on familial wisdom. In dealing with issues of sexuality, tolerance and inclusion should be the watchwords for Hindus. No sexual orientation is condemned, although the catechism acknowledges that heterosexuality is politically and socially more advantageous than being gay. While marriage and child-rearing are expected, the existence and worth of gay people is also accepted. Above all, self-knowledge and self-love are taught to the young, in contrast with the Western traditions of self-hatred and rejection.

from *Dancing With Siva*, Published by The Himalayan Academy

Sloka 74
The purpose of sexual union is to express and foster love's beautiful intimacy and to draw husband and wife together for procreation. While offering community guidance, Hinduism does not legislate sexual matters. Aum.

Bhashya
Sexual intercourse is a natural reproductive function, a part of the instinctive nature, and its pleasures draw man and woman together that a child may be conceived. It also serves through its intimacy to express and nurture love. It is love which endows sexual intercourse with its higher qualities, transforming

it from an animal function to human fulfillment. Intensely personal matters of sex as they affect the family or individual are not legislated, but left to the judgment of those involved, subject to community laws and customs.

Hinduism neither condones nor condemns birth control, sterilization, masturbation, homosexuality, petting, polygamy, or pornography. It does not exclude or draw harsh conclusions against any part of human nature, though scripture prohibits adultery and forbids abortion except to save a mother's life. Advice in such matters should be sought from parents, elders, and spiritual leaders. The only rigid rule is wisdom, guided by tradition and virtue. The *Vedas* beseech, "May all the divine powers together with the waters join our two hearts in one! May the Messenger, the Creator, and the holy Obedience unite us." Aum Namah Sivaya.

Sloka 75
Wisdom demands that the intimacies of sexual intercourse be confined to marriage....

Bhashya
...A healthy, unrepressed attitude should be kept regarding sexual matters. Boys and girls must be taught to value and protect their chastity as a sacred treasure, and to save the special gift of intimacy for their spouse....

Sloka 84
All but the rare few inclined to monastic life should be encouraged to marry and schooled in the skills they will need to fulfill [their duty]. Young boys destined to be monsatics should be raised as their *satguru's* progeny. Aum.

Bhashya
...Generally, children should be taught to follow and prepare themselves for the householder path....Sons and daughters who are gay may not benefit from marriage, and should be taught to remain loyal in relationships, and be prepared to cope with community challenges....

HADRIAN AND ANTINOUS

For many centuries, Greece and Rome dominated the Mediterranean world. By the beginning of the Common Era, the spreading Roman Empire had assimilated the old Alexandrine territories, and with them, the tastes and values of the pederastic Greek culture, which shaped the sensibilities of the Empire until the ascendancy of the Christian church. The complex and complementary relationship between Greece and Rome is mirrored in the intense love relationship between Emperor Hadrian and Antinuous, which reached its climax when the Emperor deified Antinuous following the youth's death in the year 130.

Born in Bythnion around the year 110 of the common era, Antinuous was a beautiful adolescent when he first caught the eye of the Emperor of the western world. Hadrian was already in his late forties by the time the two met; their sexual chemistry appears to have been mutual, electric, and immediate. Antinuous became Hadrian's favorite, sharing the Emperor's bed and his life. For a period of a little less than a decade, the two men were inseparable, much to the disgrace of Hadrian's legal wife, the childless and spiteful Sabina. Imperial art and literature of the time shows the men in a variety of guises and activities, particularly hunting, a sport the two enjoyed immensely.

In the course of their relationship, Antinuous matured from an extraordinarily sweet and beautiful youth into an intelligent and well-muscled young man. The Greeks referred to the visible maturation of a youth, the growth of his beard and body hair, as "clouds hiding the sun". It was shortly after the Emperor's young lover had reached this stage of his development, and just after his hair had been cut short in the style favored by mature men of the period, that Antinuous drowned mysteriously in the Nile during an Imperial visit to the province of Egypt.

Egyptian custom decreed that all drowning victims in the Nile automatically assumed a type of minor divinity, and so Antinuous was proclaimed a god. Within a year Hadrian returned to Rome, where he officially proclaimed Antinuous as a Roman god. While still deeply mourning the loss of his beloved, the Emperor had realized the political significance of the Greek youth's death, and from the tragedy forged a unifying cult of worship in the previously divided Greek city-states. Hadrian and Antinuous together built a unified Greek nation, a feat which the warring city-states themselves had never achieved. Despite other great accomplishment as Emperor, Hadrian spent the last eight years of his life mourning Antinuous.

To commemorate their great love, Hadrian worked relentlessly to build monuments and institutions to his beloved. The Emperor founded the Greek-Egyptian city Antinoopolis on the banks of the Nile near where Antinuous had died; commissioned nearly two thousand likenesses, carved from various stone materials; erected temples and altars to the new young god all over Asia Minor; and established schools, gymnasiums, panhellenic games and contests in his name. Official Roman coins were struck in all parts of the Empire except Rome to commemorate the beautiful young man. One of many distinctions relating to Antinuous is that, of all the citizens of the Roman Empire, his is the only non-Imperial image ever to have been struck on coins of the realm. Medallions bearing Antinuous' image were issued and quickly became religious icons.

The early Christians, struggling at the time to win converts to their new religion, were dismayed and disgusted at the deification of Antinuous, whose cult, in many cities of the Empire, eclipsed the cult of the dead Jesus. Records and artifacts show that for centuries the likeness of Antinuous was worn as a talisman against evil, kept as a bust in homes and businesses, and worshipped publicly throughout the Mediterranean world. It was not until the ascendancy of Christianity three hundred years later that the cult was extinguished through vigorous and systematic persecution by the Church.

Today, rows of broken and scavenged marble columns in the Egyptian desert mark the site where the city of Antinoopolis once bustled alongside the Nile; the hundreds of magnificent busts of Antinuous went long ago, cooked for fuel in the coke ovens. There remain now fewer than two hundred friezes, busts, statues, and reliefs carved in the image of Hadrian's beloved; many of those still in existence are hoarded out of sight within the Vatican.

Ultimately, Hadrian immortalized his beloved not through imperial deification, but by engendering the finest surviving artistic accomplishments of Imperial Roman sculpture in the likeness of Antinuous.

For a detailed and fascinating examination of the love story of Hadrian and Antinuous, see Royston Lambert's *Beloved and God*.

N.126

PART TWO: LITERATURE

Homer

At the dawn of Western literature, completely shrouded in the twilight of time, looms the mysterious figure of the Greek poet Homer. Before him, the craft of writing was a mundane clerical occupation; since Homer, to paraphrase Oscar Wilde, poet-singers have created the world for the dreamer.

Nearly nothing is known for certain about the supposed author of *The Iliad* and its sequel, *The Odyssey.* His place of birth is said to be one of seven different cities in Asia Minor; the date of his birth sometime between the twelfth and ninth century before the common era. Debate rages as to whether the author is one man or many, about the source of the material, about the accuracy and political bias of the facts. But there is no debate regarding the quality of the poems themselves, which remain the greatest epic poems ever produced.

Homer's masterpieces, the *Iliad* and the *Odyssey*, are constructed from parts of a much larger oral tradition narrating the conflict that we call the Trojan War. Lesser works, some written later, fill in the gaps of this complex story. But each of the volumes can be read as a self-contained epic, complete with its own characters, plot, and resolution. In this way, the cycle of poems might be compared to a movie, such the *Star Wars* trilogy.

The *Iliad* tells the story of a war waged to retrieve Helen, who has eloped with the Trojan prince, Paris. Already encamped before the walls of Troy for nine years when the *Iliad* begins, the Greeks are weary of the siege, and many are ready to abandon Helen and return home. But the gods and goddesses on Mount Olympus have decreed that this will not happen until certain key events come to pass; the Olympians interfere throughout the epic, trying to help their favorites, and destroy those they hate.

The central character of the *Iliad* is the beautiful and gigantic Akhilleus, prince of the Myrmidons and champion of the Akhaians. Born of a divine mother and a mortal father, Akhilleus has been blessed with superior skill and a charmed

---

life on the battle field.[1] Psychologically, Akhilleus has one weak spot: his intense love for his soul mate, Patróklos. In the early sections of the poem, a feud develops between Akhilleus and Agamemnon, the king of the Akhaians. As a result, Akhilleus refuses to fight during a key battle, and Patróklos, wearing Akhilleus' armor, enters the fray, only to be slain by the Trojan champion, Hektor.

It is the death in pitched battle of Akhilleus' lover, Patróklos "—his lover," Plato declares, "and not his love…",[2] which motivates Akhilleus' terrible vengeance against Hektor and the Trojans. While his savage and brutal revenge belongs to a savage and long-gone age, Akhilleus' shock and rage resonate deeply in today's gay community. Akhilleus' interior journey through wastelands of grief and mourning is in many ways more gripping and compelling than any battle scenes in the *Iliad*.

The concepts, emotions, characters and situations of these poems inspire and echo within many great works of literature. Milton's *Paradise Lost* imitates the *Iliad's* form and style; Milton's works constantly alludes to Homer. Virgil's *Aeniad* is an attempt to secure for Rome the same literary glory bestowed by the *Iliad* on Greece. Ovid alludes constantly to Homer in his works, as does Plato; the story of David and Jonathan imitates the story of Patróklos and Akhilleus; Oscar Wilde invokes and dissects Homer's writing in his poetic prose argument, *The Critic as Artist*. All of the subsequent epic poetry of the Mediterranean world is patterned, to some degree, after Homer, and most of classical Western literature is descended, in one way or another, from Homer's works.

Yet, perhaps because a gay relationship forms the heart of the *Iliad,* Homer is no longer widely taught in America's public schools.

from *The Iliad, Book Eighteen:*

"Here's desolation,
son of Pêleus, the worst news for you—
would god it hadn't happened!—Lord Patróklos

fell, and they are fighting over his body,
stripped of armor. Hektor has your gear."

A black stormcloud of pain shrouded Akhilleus.
On his bowed head he scattered dust and ash
in handfuls and befouled his beautiful face,
letting black ash sift onto his fragrant khiton.[3]
Then in the dust he stretched his giant length
and tore his hair with both hands.
                From the hut
the women who had been the spoils of war to him
and to Patróklos flocked in haste around him,
crying aloud in grief. All beat their breasts,
and trembling came upon their knees.
                Antílokhos
wept where he stood, bending to hold the hero's
hands when groaning shook his heart: he feared
the man might use sharp iron to slash his throat.
And now Akhilleus gave a dreadful cry.
                Her ladyship
his mother heard him, in the depths offshore
lolling near her ancient father....Bending near
her groaning son, the gentle goddess wailed
and took his head between her hands in pity,
saying softly:
                "Child, why are you weeping?
What great sorrow came to you?..."
                The great runner
groaned and answered:
                "...My greatest friend
is gone: Patróklos, comrade in arms, whom I
held dear above all others—dear as myself—
now gone; lost. Hektor cut him down, despoiled him
of my own arms, massive and fine, a wonder
in all men's eyes...
"I must reject this life, my heart tells me,
reject the world of men,
if Hektor does not feel my battering spear

tear the life out of him, making him pay
in his own blood for the slaughter of Patróklos!"

Letting a tear fall, Thetis said:
                    "You'll be
swift to meet your end, child, as you say:
your doom comes close on the heels of Hektor's own."

Akhilleus the great runner ground his teeth
and said:
                    "May it come quickly. As things were,
I could not help my friend in his extremity.
Far from his home he died; he needed me
to shield him or to parry the death stroke.
For me there's no return to my own country.
Not the slightest gleam of hope did I
afford Patróklos or the other men
whom Hektor overpowered. Here I sat,
my weight a useless burden to the earth;
and I am one who has no peer in war
among Akhaian captains—though in council
there are wiser....

"Now I must go to look for the destroyer
of my great friend. I shall confront the dark
drear spirit of death at any hour Zeus
and the other gods may wish to make an end.
Not even Hêraklês escaped that terror...."

                    Akhilleus,
whom Zeus loved, now rose. Around his shoulders
Athêna hung her shield, like a thunderhead
with trailing fringe. Goddess of goddesses,
she bound his head with golden cloud, and made
his very body blaze with fiery light....
...so the baleful radiance from Akhilleus
lit the sky. Moving from the parapet
to moat, without a nod for the Akhaians,

keeping clear, in deference to his mother,
he halted and gave tongue. Not far from him
Athêna shrieked. The great sound shocked the Trojans
into tumult, as a trumpet blown
by savage foe shocks an encircled town,
so harsh and clarion was Akhilleus' cry.
The hearts of men quailed, hearing that brazen voice.
Teams, foreknowing danger, turned their cars
and charioteers blanched, seeing unearthly fire,
kindled by the grey-eyed goddess Athêna,
brilliant over Akhilleus. Three great cries
he gave above the moat. Three times they shuddered,
whirling backward, Trojans and allies,
and twelve good men took mortal hurt
from cars and weapons in the rank behind.
Now the Akhaians leapt at the chance
to bear Patróklos' body out of range.
They placed it on his bed,
and old companions there with brimming eyes
surrounded him. Into their midst Akhilleus
came then, and he wept hot tears to see
his faithful friend, torn by the sharp spearhead,
lying cold upon his cot. Alas,
the man he sent to war with team and chariot
he could not welcome back alive.
                Her majesty,
wide-eyed Hêra, made the reluctant sun,
unwearied, sink in the streams of Ocean.
Down he dropped, and the Akhaian soldiers
broke off combat, resting from the war.
The Trojans, too, retired....

...all night long, the Akhaians mourned Patróklos.
Akhilleus led them in their lamentation,
laying those hands deadly to enemies
upon the breast of his old friend, with groans
at every breath, bereft as a lioness
whose whelps a hunter seized out of a thicket;

late in returning, she will grieve, and roam
through many meandering valleys on his track
in hope of finding him; heart-stinging anger
carries her away. Now with a groan
he cried out to the Myrmidons:
                    "Ah, god,
what empty prophesy I made that day
to cheer Menoites in his mégaron![4]
I promised him his honored son, brought back
to Opoeis, as pillager of Ilion
bearing his share of spoils.
But Zeus will not fulfill what men design,
not all of it. Both he and I were destined
to stain the same earth dark red here at Troy.
No going home for me; no welcome there
from Pêleus, master of horse, or from my mother,
Thetis. Here the earth will hold me under.
Therefore, as I must follow you into the grave,
I will not give you burial, Patróklos,
until I carry back the gear and head
of him who killed you, noble friend.
Before your funeral pyre I'll cut the throats
of twelve resplendent children of the Trojans—
that is my murdering fury at your death...."

With this Akhilleus called the company
to place over the campfire a big tripod
and bathe Patróklos of his clotted blood.
Setting the tripod and cauldron upon the blaze
they poured it full, and fed the fire beneath,
and flames licked round the belly of the vessel
until the water warmed and bubbled up
in the bright bronze. They bathed him then and took
sweet oil for his annointing, laying nard[5]
in the open wounds, on his bed they placed him,
covering him with fine linen head to foot,
and a white shroud over it.
                    So all that night

beside Akhilleus the great runner,
the Myrmidons held mourning for Patróklos....

from Book Nineteen:

Dawn in her yellow robe rose in the east
out of the flowing Ocean, bringing light
for deathless gods and mortal men. And Thetis
brought to the beach her gifts from the god of fire.
She found her dear son lying beside Patróklos,
wailing, while his men stood by
in tears around him. Now amid that throng
the lovely goddess bent to touch his shoulder
and said to him:
        "Ah, child, let him lie dead,
for all our grief and pain we must allow it;
he fell by the gods' will.
But you, now—take the war-gear from Hêphaistos.
No man ever bore upon his shoulders
gear so magnificent."
        And she laid the armor
down before Akhilleus, clanging loud
in all its various glories. Myrmidons
began to tremble at the sound, and dared not
look straight at the armor; their knees shook.
But anger entered Akhilleus as he gazed,
his eyes grown wide and bright as blazing fire,
with fierce joy as he handled the god's gifts.
After appraising them in delight
he spoke out to his mother swiftly:
                "Mother,
these the god gave are miraculous arms,
handiwork of immortals, plainly—far
beyond the craft of men. I'll wear them!
Only, I feel the dread that while I fight
black carrion flies may settle on Patróklos'
wounds, where spearheads marked him, and I fear
they may breed maggots to defile the corpse,

now life is torn from it. He may rot."

But silvery footed Thetis answered:
                    "Child,
You must not let that prey on you. I'll find
a way to shield him from the black fly hordes
that eat the bodies of men killed in battle.
Though he should lie unburied a long year,
his flesh will be intact and firm. Now, though,
for your part, call the Akhaians to assembly.
Tell them your anger against Agamemnon
is over and done with!
After that, at once
put on your gear, prepare your heart, for war!"

Her promise gave her son whole-hearted valor.
Then, turning to Patróklos, she instilled
red nectar and ambrosia in his nostrils
to keep his body whole.…
                    Reflected
glintings flashed to heaven, as the plain
in all directions shone with the glare of bronze
and shook with the trampling of feet. Among them
Prince Akhilleus armed. One heard his teeth
grind hard together, and his eyes blazed out
like licking fire, for unbearable pain
had fixed upon his heart. Raging at Trojans,
he buckled on the arms Hêphaistos had forged.…
Now from his spear-case he withdrew a spear—
his father's—weighty, long, and tough. No other
Akhaian had the strength to handle it,
this great Pêlian shaft
of ashwood, given his father by the centaur
Kheiron from the chest of Pelion
to be the death of heroes.…

from Book Twenty:
                    …Akhilleus

went into that battle wild to engage
great Hektor, son of Priam, with whose blood
his great heart and soul desired to glut the wargod....

from Book Twenty-two:

Hektor stood firm, as huge Akhilleus neared.
           ...Hektor, grim
and narrow-eyed, refused to yield. He leaned
his brilliant shield against a spur of wall
and in his brave heart bitterly reflected:
"Here I am badly caught....
           ...troops have perished for my foolish pride,
I am ashamed to face townsmen and women.
Someone inferior to me may say:
'He kept his pride and lost his men, this Hektor!'
So it will go. Better, when that time comes,
that I appear as he who killed Akhilleus
man to man, or else that I went down
before him honorably for the city's sake...."
           Now close at hand
Akhilleus like the implacable god of war
came on with blowing crest, hefting the dreaded
beam of Pêlian ash on his right shoulder.
Bronze light played around him, like the glare
of a great fire, or the great sun rising,
and Hektor, as he watched, began to tremble.
Then he could hold his ground no more. He ran,
leaving the gate behind him, with Akhilleus
hard on his heels, sure of his own speed.
When that most lightening-like of birds, a hawk
bred on a mountain, swoops upon a dove,
the quarry dips in terror, but the hunter,
screaming, slips behind and gains upon it,
passionate for prey. Just so, Akhilleus
murderously cleft the air, as Hektor
ran with flashing knees along the wall.
They passed the lookout point, the wild fig-tree

with wind in all its leaves, then veered away
along the curving wagon road, and came
to where the double fountains well, the source
of eddying Skamánder....
                    Past these
the two men ran, pursuer and pursued,
and he who fled was noble, he behind
a greater man by far. They ran full speed,
and not for bull's hide or a ritual beast
or any prize that men compete for: no,
but for the life of Hektor, tamer of horses.
            ...three times these two
at full speed made their course round Priam's town,
as all the gods looked on....
            Hektor could not shake off
the great runner, Akhilleus. Every time
he tried to sprint hard for the Dardan gates
under the towers, hoping men could help him,
sending missiles down, Akhilleus loomed
to cut him off and turn him toward the plain,
as he himself ran always near the city.
As in a dream a man chasing another
cannot catch him, nor can he in flight
escape from his pursuer, so Akhilleus
could not by his swiftness overtake him,
nor could Hektor pull away. How could he
run so long from death, had not Apollo
for the last time, the very last time, come near
to give him stamina and speed?
                    Akhilleus
shook his head at the rest of the Akhaians
allowing none to shoot or cast at Hektor—
none to forestall him, and win the honor.
But when, for the fourth time, they reached the springs,
the Father poised his golden scales. He placed
two shapes of death, death prone and cold, upon them,
one of Akhilleus, one of the horseman, Hektor,
and held the midpoint, pulling upward. Down

sank Hektor's fatal day, the pan went down
toward under-gloom, and Phoebus Apollo left him.

…And when at last the two men faced each other,
Hektor was the first to speak. He said:

"I will no longer fear you as before,
son of Pêleus, though I ran from you
round Priam's town three times and could not face you.
Now my soul would have me stand and fight,
whether I kill you or am killed. So come,
we'll summon gods here as our witnesses,
none higher, arbiters of a pact: I swear
that, terrible as you are,
I'll not insult your corpse should Zeus allow me
victory in the end, your life as prize.
Once I have your gear I'll give your body
back to the Akhaians. Grant me too, this grace."

But swift Akhilleus frowned at him and said:

"Hektor, I'll have no talk of pacts with you,
forever unforgiven as you are.
As between men and lions there are none,
no concord between wolves and sheep, but all
hold one another hateful through and through,
so there can be no courtesy between us,
no sworn truce, till one of us is down
and glutting with his blood the war god Arês.
Summon up what skills you have. By god,
you'd better be a spearman and a fighter!
Now there is no way out. Pallas Athêna
will have the upper hand of you. The weapon
belongs to me. You'll pay the reckoning
in full for all the pain my men have borne,
who met death by your spear."

He twirled and cast

his shaft with its long shadow. Splendid Hektor,
keeping his eye upon the point, eluded it
by ducking at the instant of the cast,
so shaft and bronze shank passed him overhead
and punched into the earth. But unperceived
by Hektor, Pallas Athêna plucked it out
and gave it back to Akhilleus. Hektor said:

"A clean miss. Godlike as you are,
you have not yet known doom for me from Zeus.
You thought you had, by heaven. Then you turned
into a word-thrower, hoping to make me lose
my fighting heart and head in fear of you.
You cannot plant your spear between my shoulders
while I am running. If you have the gift,
just put it through my chest as I come forward.
Now it's for you to dodge my own. Would god
you'd give the whole shaft lodging in your body!
War for the Trojans would be eased
if you were blotted out, bane that you are."

With this he twirled his long spear-shaft and cast it,
hitting his enemy mid-shield, but off
and away the spear rebounded. Furious
that he had lost it, made his throw for nothing,
Hektor stood bemused....
                    Now in his heart
the Trojan realized the truth and said:

"This is the end. The gods are calling deathward...
Death is near, and black, not at a distance,
not to be evaded. Long ago
this hour must have been to Zeus' liking
and to the liking of his archer son.
They have been well disposed before, but now
the appointed time's upon me. Still, I would not
die without delivering a stroke,
or die ingloriously, but in some action

memorable to men in days to come."

With this he drew the whetted blade that hung
upon his left flank, ponderous and long,
collecting all his might the way an eagle
narrows himself to dive through shady cloud
and strike a lamb or cowering hare: so Hektor
lanced ahead and swung his whetted blade.
Akhilleus with wild fury in his heart
pulled in upon his chest his beautiful shield—
his helmet with four burnished metal ridges
nodding above it, and the golden crest
Hêphaistos locked there tossing in the wind.
Conspicuous as the evening star that comes,
amid the first in heaven, at fall of night,
and stands most lovely in the west, so shone
in sunlight the fine pointed spear
Akhilleus poised in his right hand, with deadly
aim at Hektor, at the skin where most
it lay exposed. But nearly all was covered
by the bronze gear he took from slain Patróklos,
showing only, where his collarbones
divided neck and shoulders, the bare throat
where the destruction of life is quickest.
Here, then, as the Trojan charged, Akhilleus
drove his spear straight through the tender neck,
but did not cut the windpipe, leaving Hektor
able to speak and to respond. He fell
aside into the dust. And Prince Akhilleus
now exulted:
   "Hektor, had you thought
that you could kill Patróklos and be safe?
Nothing to dread from me; I was not there.
All childishness. Though distant then, Patróklos'
comrade in arms was greater far than he—
and it is I who had been left behind
that day beside the deepsea ships who now
have made your knees give way. The dogs and kites

will rip your body. His will lie in honor
when the Akhaians give him funeral."

Hektor, barely whispering, replied:

"I beg you by your soul and by your parents,
do not let the dogs feed on me
in your encampment by the ships. Accept
the bronze and gold my father will provide
as gifts, my father and her ladyship
my mother. Let them have my body back,
so that our men and women may accord me
decency of fire when I am dead."

Akhilleus the great runner scowled and said:

"Beg me no beggary by soul or parents,
whining dog! Would god my passion drove me
to slaughter you and eat you raw, you've caused
such agony to me! No man exists
who could defend you from the carrion pack—
not if they spread for me ten times your ransom,
twenty times, promised me more as well;
aye, not if Priam, son of Dárdanos,
tells them to buy you for your weight in gold!
You'll have no bed of death, nor will you be
laid out and mourned by her who gave you birth.
Dogs and birds will have you, every scrap."

Then at the point of death Lord Hektor said:

"I see you now for what you are. No chance
to win you over. Iron in your breast
your heart is. Think a bit though: this may be
a thing the gods in anger will hold against you
on that day when Paris and Apollo
destroy you at the Gates, great as you are."

Even as he spoke, the end came, and death hid him;
spirit from body fluttered to the aftergloom,
bewailing fate that made her leave his youth
and manhood in the world. And as he died
Akhilleus spoke again. He said:

"Die, make an end. I shall accept my own
whenever Zeus and the other gods desire."

…When the great master of pursuit, Akhilleus,
had the body stripped, he stood among them,
saying swiftly:

"Friends, my lords and captains of the Argives…
down by the ships Patróklos' body lies
unwept, unburied. I shall not forget him
while I can keep my feet among the living.
If in the dead world they forget the dead,
I say there, too, I shall remember him,
my friend. Men of Akhaia, lift a song!
Down to the ships we go, and take this body,
our glory. We have beaten Hektor down,
to whom as to a god the Trojans prayed."

Indeed, he had in mind for Hektor's body
outrage and shame. Behind both feet he pierced
the tendons, heel to ankle. Rawhide cords
he drew through both and lashed them to his chariot,
letting the man's head trail. Stepping aboard,
bearing the great trophy of the arms,
he shook the reins, and whipped the team ahead
into a willing run. A dustcloud rose
above the furrowing body; the dark tresses
flowed behind, and the head so princely once
lay back in dust. Zeus gave him to his enemies
to be defiled in his own fatherland.…

from Book Twenty-three:

              ...Retiring
shoreward to the beach and Hellê's waters,
each to his ship, Akhaians turned away,
but not the Myrmidons. Akhilleus held them
undismissed, and spoke among these fighters:

"Chariot-skirmishers, friends of my heart,
we'll not unharness our good horses now
but in our war-cars filing near Patróklos
mourn him in line. That is fit honor paid
to a captain fallen. When we've gained relief
in lamentation, we can free the teams
and take our evening meal here."

              With one voice
they all cried out in sorrow, and he led them,
driving their teams with wind-blown manes three times
around the body, weeping, and among them
Thetis roused their longing to lament.
The sandy field, the gear of men grew wet
with salt tears, for they missed him bitterly,
the man who turned the battle tide. Akhilleus
led them in repeated cries of grief,
laying his deadly hands upon his friend:

"Patróklos, peace be with you in the dark
where Death commands, aye, even there. You see
I shall have soon done all I promised you:
I dragged Hektor this far, to give wild dogs
his flesh and let them rend it among themselves,
and I have brought twelve radiant sons of Troy
whose throats I'll cut, to bloody your great pyre,
such fury came upon me at your death."

Shameless abuse indeed he planned for Hektor,
and laid the body face down in the dust
beside Patróklos' bed of death. His soldiers

now unbuckled all their brazen gear,
freed the whinnying horses of their harness,
and sat down, in their hundreds, all before
Akhilleus' ship. Then to their heart's desire
he made the funeral feast....

Akhaian peers induced Akhilleus now—
barely prevailing on his grief and rage—
to visit the Lord Agamémnon;
and when they came up to the Marshal's hut
they bade the clear-voiced criers there
set out a tripod caldron on the fire,
thinking Akhilleus might wash off the blood
that stained his body. He would not hear of it,
but swore:
       "By Zeus, I will not! By that god
best and all-highest, it is not in order
to bring hot water near me, till I lay
Patróklos on his pyre, and heap his barrow,
and shear my hair. No burden like this grief
will come a second time upon my heart,
while I remain among the living.
           Now,
by heaven, we'll consent to the grim feast.
At first light turn the men out, my Lord Marshal,
to bring in all the firewood required
that the dead man may reach the gloomy west;
then let strong fire hide and consume the corpse;
and let the troops return to duty."

So he spoke, and they listened and obeyed him...
but on the beach near the wash and ebb
Akhilleus lay down groaning among his men,
his Myrmidons, on a bare open place
where breakers roll in spume upon the shore.
Pursuing Hektor around windy Troy
he had worn out his legs. Now restful floods
of sleep, dissolving heartache, came upon him,

and soon forlorn Patróklos' shade came near—
a perfect likeness of the man, in height,
fine eyes, and voice, and dressed in his own fashion.
The image stood above him and addressed him:

"Sleeping so? Thou hast forgotten me,
Akhilleus. Never was I uncared for
in life but am in death. Accord me burial
in all haste: let me pass the gates of Death.
Shades that are images of used-up men
motion me away, will not receive me
among their hosts beyond the river. I wander
about the wide gates and the hall of Death.
Give me your hand. I sorrow.
When thou shalt have allotted me my fire
I will not fare here from the dark again.
As living men we'll no more sit apart
from our companions, making plans. The day
of wrath appointed for me at my birth
engulfed and took me down. Thou too, Akhilleus,
face iron destiny, godlike as thou art,
to die under the wall of highborn Trojans.
One more message, one behest, I leave thee:
not to inter my bones apart from thine
but close together, as we grew together,
in thy family's hall....
So may the same urn hide our bones, the one
of gold your gracious mother gave."

                    Akhilleus
spoke in answer, saying:

                    "Dear old friend,
why comest hither, and why these demands?
I shall bring all to pass for thee; I shall
comply with all thy bidding. Only stand
nearer to me. For this little time
may we embrace and take our fill of tears."

He stretched his arms out but took hold of nothing,
as into earth Patróklos' shade like smoke
retreated with a faint cry. Then Akhilleus
rose in wonderment and clapped his hands,
and slowly said:

      "A wisp of life remains
in the under-gloom of Death: a visible form,
though no heart beats within it. All this night
the shade of poor Patróklos bent above me
grieving and weeping, charging me with tasks.
It seemed to the life the very man."
                At this
the Myrmidons were stirred again to weep.
Then Dawn with rose-red fingers in the east
began to glow upon them as they mourned
around the pitiful body.
              Agamémnon
ordered out mules and men from every hut
to forage firewood....On the shore they stacked
their burdens in a woodpile, where Akhilleus
planned Patróklos' barrow and his own;
then, having heaped a four-square mass of timber,
all sat down together. Now Akhilleus ordered
his veteran Myrmidons to arm
and yoke their horses to the chariots.
They rose and put their gear on. Chariot fighters
mounted with drivers in their cars, and these
moved out ahead; behind, a cloud of infantry
followed. In between, his old companions
bore Patróklos, covering the corpse
with locks of hair they sheared off and let fall.
Akhilleus held the head in grief; his friend
he would consign now to the world of Death.
When they had reached the place Akhilleus chose
they put the body down and built the pyre
of timber, high as they could wish. Akhilleus

turned to another duty now. Apart
from the pyre he stood and cut the red-gold hair
that he had grown for the river Sperkheios.
Gazing over the winedark sea in pain,
he said:

"Sperkheios, Pêleus my father's vow
to you meant nothing, that on my return
I'd cut my hair as an offering to you,
along with fifty sheep ungelded, slain
at your headwaters, where your park and alter
fragrant with incense are. The old man swore it,
but you would not fulfill what he desired.
Now, as I shall not see my fatherland,
I would confer my hair upon the soldier
Patróklos."

And he closed his dear friend's hands
upon it, moving all to weep again.
The sun would have gone down upon their weeping
had not Akhilleus quickly turned and said
to Agamémnon:

"Sir, troops act at once
on your command. Men may grow sick of tears.
Dismiss these from the pyre to make a meal,
and we who are closest to the dead will care
for what is to be done now. Let each captain
stay with us here."

On hearing this, the Marshal
Agamémnon made the troops disperse
at once to their own ships. Close friends remained.
They added timber and enlarged the pyre
to a hundred feet a side. On top of it
with heavy hearts they laid the dead man down....
Then in the midst [Akhilleus] thrust the pitiless might
of fire to feed..., and cried
upon his dead companion:

"Peace be with you

even in the dark where Death commands, Patróklos.
Everything has been finished as I promised.
Fire will devour twelve noble sons of Troy
along with you, but I will not restore
Hektor to Priam; he shall not be eaten
by fire, but by wild dogs."
                That was his boast,
but no dogs nosed at Hektor: Zeus' daughter
Aphrodítê kept them from his body
day and night....
          ...The north and west winds
issued with a wondrous cry, both driving
cloud before them. Over open sea...they came
and fell upon the pyre. The flame roared,
blazing terribly, and all night long
they joined to toss the crest of fire high
with keening blasts. And all night long Akhilleus
dipped up wine from a golden bowl and poured
his double cupfuls down, soaking the earth,
and calling Patróklos' feeble shade. He mourned him
as a father mourns a newly married son
whose death is anguish to his kin. Just so
Akhilleus mourned his friend and gave his bones
to the great flame to be devoured; with dragging
steps and groans he moved about the pyre.
Now when the star of morning eastward rose
to herald daylight on the earth, and Dawn
came after, yellow-robed, above the sea,
the pyre died down, the flame sank, and the winds
departed, veering homeward once again
by sea for Thrace, as the groundswell heaved and foamed.
Akhilleus left the pyre and lay down spent...

from Book Twenty-four:

          …Men dispersed
and turned their thoughts to supper in their quarters,
then to the boon of slumber. But Akhilleus
thought of his friend, and sleep that quiets all things
would not take hold of him. He tossed and turned
remembering with pain Patróklos courage,
his buoyant heart; how in his company
he fought out many a rough day full of danger,
cutting through ranks in war and the bitter sea.
With memory his eyes grew wet. He lay
on his right side, then on his back, and then
face downward—but at last he rose, to wander
distractedly along the line of surf.
This for eleven nights. The first dawn, brightening
sea and shore, became familiar to him,
as at that hour he yoked his team, with Hektor
tied behind, to drag him out, three times
around Patróklos' tomb.…

1 Legends tell that Akhilleus' mother Thetis, a daughter of the god Poseidon, rendered her son invulnerable by dipped him as an infant into a river. Unfortunately, the spot where she held his heel was not covered by the magic charm. Akhilleus was killed when Paris shot a poisoned arrow into his vulnerable heel.

2 Jowett, Princeton, 1942. This distinction between lover and beloved was very important to Hellenic men, and vital to their Roman counterparts. In the Roman culture, there was some social disgrace in an older male taking the passive role in anal intercourse, especially with a younger man. See e.g. Martial Book Twelve, Epigrams 35, 42 below.

3 knee-length Greek tunic.

4 great hall.

5 a fragrant ointment used by the ancients.

Oscar Wilde

(1854-1900)

The great gay writer of the Victorian era, Oscar Wilde, was ruined by the disclosure of his homoerotic orientation. His lasting fame stems partly from his wonderful writing, and partly from his spectacular disgrace. A powerful force in Victorian society, Wilde enjoyed the company of the highest social circles. Oscar once quipped that he had given only his talent to his work: his genius he spent on his life. Other leading figures of his own time confirmed that Wilde the writer was eclipsed by Wilde, the storyteller. George Bernard Shaw acknowledged Wilde as the greatest talker he had ever heard, which is no small praise from a fellow Irishman.

Wilde's plays, such as *Lady Windemere's Fan* and *The Importance Of Being Earnest,* were enormously popular in their day. His short stories and poems, successful in lesser degrees, also aroused much praise, as did his only novel, *The Picture of Dorian Gray.* Many of Wilde's writings feature thinly disguised gay characters and situations; these works, and his own personal correspondence, were used against Wilde in court.

Wilde himself created the scandal of the age when he sued the Marquis of Queensberry for slandering him as a homosexual. Following two of the most sensationally publicized trials of his day (1895), Wilde was convicted of sodomy, and sentenced to two years in prison at hard labor. There he wrote his broken hearted masterpiece, *The Ballad of Reading Gaol; De Profundis,* also written in prison, is Wilde's autobiographical attempt to come to grips with his disgrace. He emerged from prison a broken man, lived under an assumed name in Paris for three years, and died in obscurity.

Due to the constraints of Victorian England, Oscar Wilde never composed anything that we today would consider gay literature. But Wilde's writings are steeped with references to classical homoerotic works such as the *Iliad,* and all of his works are infused with the finest of gay sensibilities.

from *The Critic as Artist:*

...When man acts he is a puppet. When he describes he is a poet. The whole secret lies in that. It was easy enough on the sandy plains by windy Ilion to send the notched arrow from the painted bow, or to hurl against the shield of hide and flame-like brass the long ash-handled spear....But what of those who wrote about these things? What of those who gave them reality, and made them live forever? Are they not greater than the men and women they sing of?...

Lucian tells us how in the dim underworld Menippus saw the bleaching skull of Helen, and marveled that it was for so grim a favor that all those horned ships were launched, those beautiful mailed men laid low, those towered cities brought to dust. Yet, every day the swan-like daughter of Leda[1] comes out on the battlements, and looks down on the tide of war. The greybeards wonder at her loveliness, and she stands by the side of the king. In her bed-chamber of stained ivory lies her leman.[2] He is polishing his dainty armor, and combing the scarlet plume. With squire and page, her husband passes from tent to tent. She can see his bright hair, and hears, or fancies that she hears, that clear cold voice. In the courtyard below, the son of Priam is buckling on his brazen cuirass. The white arms of Andromache are around his neck. He sets his helmet on the ground, lest their babe should be frightened. Behind the embroidered curtain of his pavilion sits Akhilleus, in perfumed raiment, while in harness of gilt and silver the friend of his soul[3] arrays himself to go forth to the fight. From a curiously carved chest that his mother Thetis had brought to his shipside, the Lord of the Myrmidons takes out that mystic chalice that the lip of man had never touched, and cleanses it with brimstone, and with water cools it, and, having washed his hands, fills with black wine its burnished hollow, and spills the thick grape-blood on the ground in honor of Him whom at Dodona[4] barefooted prophets worshipped, and prays to Him, and knows not that he prays in vain, and that by the hands of two knights of Troy , Panthous' son, Euphorbus, whose love-locks were looped with gold, and the Priamid, the lion-hearted, Patróklos, the comrade of comrades, must meet his doom. Phantoms, are they? Heroes of mist and mountain? Shadows in a song? No; they are real. Action! What is action? It dies at the moment of it's energy. It is a base concession to fact. The world is made by the singer for the dreamer....

It is so in truth. On the moldering citadel of Troy lies the lizard like a thing of green bronze. The owl has built her nest in the palace of Priam. Over the empty plain wander shepherd and goatherd with their flocks, and where, on the wine-surfaced, oily sea, the "wine-dark sea" as Homer calls it, copper prowed and streaked with vermillion, the great galleys of the Danaoi came in their gleaming crescent, the lonely tunny-fisher sits in his little boat and watches the bobbing corks of his net. Yet, every morning the doors of the city are thrown open, and on foot, or in horse-drawn chariot, the warriors go forth to battle, and mock their enemies from behind their iron masks. All day the fight rages, and when night comes, the torches gleam by their tent, and the cresset[5] burns in the hall.

Those who live in marble or on painted panel know of life but a single exquisite instant, eternal indeed in its beauty, but limited to one note of passion or one mood of calm. Those whom the poet makes live have their myriad emotions of joy and terror, of courage and despair, of pleasure and of suffering. But those who walk in epos,[6] drama or romance, see through the laboring months the young moons wax and wane, and watch the night from evening unto morningstar, and from sunrise unto sunsetting can note the shifting day with all its gold and shadow....

The statue is concentrated to one moment of perfection. The image stained upon canvas possesses no spiritual element of growth or change. If they know nothing of death, it is because they know little of life, for the secrets of life and death belong to those, and those only, whom the sequence of life affects, and who possess not merely the present but the future, and can rise or fall from a past of glory or of shame. Movement, that problem of the visible arts, can be truly realized by Literature alone. It is Literature that shows us the body in its swiftness and the soul in its unrest....

Hélas

To drift with every passion till my soul
Is a stringed lute on which all winds can play,
Is it for this that I have given away
Mine ancient wisdom, and austere control?
Methinks my life is a twice-written scroll
Scrawled over on some boyish holiday
With idle songs for pipe and virelay,[7]
Which do but mar the secret of the whole.
Surely there was a time I might have trod
The sunlit heights, and from life's dissonance
Struck one clear chord to reach the ears of God:
Is that time dead? lo! with a little rod
I did but touch the honey of romance—
And must I lose a soul's inheritance?

(1881)

from the Preface to *The Picture of Dorian Grey*

The artist is the creator of beautiful things.
To reveal art and conceal the artist is art's aim....
Those who find ugly meaning in beautiful things are corrupt
without being charming. This is a fault. Those who find beautiful meanings in beautiful things are the cultivated. For them
there is hope.
They are the elect to whom beautiful things mean only Beauty.
There is no such thing as a moral or immoral book. Books are
well written, or badly written. That is all....

(1891)

The Disciple[8]

When Narcissus died the pool of his pleasure changed from a cup of sweet waters into a cup of salt tears, and the Oreads[9] came weeping through the woodland that they might sing to the pool and give it comfort.

And when they saw that the pool had changed from a cup of sweet waters into a cup of salt tears, they loosened the green tresses of their hair and cried to the pool and said, "We do not wonder that you should mourn in this manner for Narcissus, so beautiful was he."

"But was he beautiful?" said the pool.

"Who should know that better than you?" answered the Oreads. "Us did he ever pass by, but you he sought for, and in the mirror of your waters he would mirror his own beauty."

And the pool answered, "But I loved Narcissus because, as he lay on my banks and looked down at me, in the mirror of his eyes I saw ever my own beauty mirrored."

(1893)

1 Helen was the daughter of Leda, who had coupled with Zeus while the god was disguised as a swan.

2 Paris.

3 Patróklos.

4 Seat of an ancient oracle of Zeus.

5 an iron vessel or basket used for holding an illuminant (as oil) and mounted as a torch or suspended as a lantern.

6 Epic poetry.

7 A song or short lyric in stanzas.

8 Wilde championed the "Poems in Prose", a new artform of which Narcissus is an excellent example. He had memorized several of these short poems, and could recite them on request.

9 any of the nymphs of mountains and hills in Greek mythology.

Ovid

(43 BCE—17 CE)

Publius Ovidius Naso, commonly called Ovid, perfected the elegiac style of poetry in the first century of the common era. Using as his texts the popular religious mythology of the Roman Republic, Ovid shaped stories of gods and mortals into long, skillfully narrated poems. Gay love, so common to the Greeks and Romans, is well represented in Ovid's accounts of these lusty mythological adventures.

Long considered textbook classics as well as poetic masterpieces, Ovid's *Metamorphoses* was routinely used as a model by later generations of poets. But with the ascendancy of the Christian church and the subsequent Dark Age in Europe, Ovid's liberal works fell into disrepute, remaining hidden and unread until the Renaissance revived the glories of pre-Christian Europe.

Today we are fortunate to have several modern, faithful[1] translations, which reveal the richly diverse sexuality of the mythological landscape that shaped the minds of the Greco-Roman world. The following selections from *Metamorphoses* deal with mythological characters who are transformed, in one way or another.

from *Metamorphoses:*

Narcissus

Now Narcissus was sixteen years of age, and could be taken for either boy or man; and boys and girls both sought his love, but in that slender stripling was pride so fierce no boy, no girl, could touch him....[Echo, a nymph, tried in vain to win his love. She] was not the only one on whom Narcissus had visited frustration; there were others, Naiads or Oreads, and young men also, till finally one rejected youth, in prayer, raised up his hands to Heaven: "May Narcissus love one day, so, himself, and not win over the creature whom he loves!" Nemesis heard him, goddess of Vengeance, and judged the plea was righteous.

There was a pool, silver with shining water, to which no shepherds came, no goats, no cattle, whose glass no bird, no beast, no falling leaf had ever troubled. Grass grew all around it, green from the nearby water, and with shadow no sun burned hotly down on. Here Narcissus, worn from the heat of hunting, came to rest finding the place delightful, and the spring refreshing for the thirsty.

As he tried to quench his thirst, inside him, deep within him, another thirst was growing, for he saw an image in the pool, and fell in love with that unbodied hope, and found a substance in what was only shadow. He looks in wonder charmed by himself, spellbound, and no more moving than any marble statue. Lying prone he sees his eyes, twin stars, and locks as comely as those of Bacchus or the god Apollo, smooth cheeks, and ivory neck, and the bright beauty of countenance, and a flush of color rising in the fair whiteness. Everything attracts him that makes him so attractive. Foolish boy, he wants himself, the loved becomes the lover, the seeker sought, the kindler burns. How often he tries to kiss the image in the water, dips in his arms to embrace the boy he sees there, and finds the boy, himself, elusive always, not knowing what he sees, but burning for it, the same delusion mocking his eyes and teasing.

Why try to catch an always fleeing image, poor credulous youngster? What you seek is nowhere, and if you turn away, you will take with you the boy you love. The vision is only shadow, only reflection lacking any substance. It comes with you, it stays with you, it goes away with you, if you can go away.

No thought of food, no thought of rest, can make him forsake the place. Stretched on the grass, in shadow, he watches, all unsatisfied, that image vain and illusive, and he almost drowns in his own watching eyes. He rises, just a little, enough to lift his arms in supplication to the trees around him, crying to the forest: "What love, whose love, has ever been more cruel? You woods should know: you have given many lovers places to hide and meet in; has there ever, through the long centuries, been anyone who has pined away as I do? He is charming,

I see him, but the charm and sight escape me. I love him and I cannot seem to find him! To make it worse, no sea, no road, no mountain, no city-wall, no gate, no barrier parts us but a thin film of water. He is eager for me to hold him. When my lips go down to kiss the pool, his rise, he reaches toward me. You would almost think that I could touch him—almost nothing keeps us apart. Come out, whoever you are! Why do you tease me so? Where do you go when I am reaching for you? I am surely neither so old or ugly as to scare you, and nymphs have been in love with me. You promise, I think, some hope with a look of more than friendship. You reach out arms when I do, and your smile follows my smiling; I have seen your tears when I was tearful; you nod and beckon when I do; your lips, it seems, answer when I am talking though what you say I cannot hear. I know the truth at last. He is myself! I feel it, I know my image now. I burn with love of my own self; I start the fire I suffer. What shall I do? Shall I give or take the asking? What shall I ask for? What I want is with me, my riches make me poor. If I could only escape from my own body! If I could only— how curious a prayer from any lover— be parted from my love! And now my sorrow is taking all my strength away; I know I have not long to live, I shall die early, and death is not so terrible, since it takes my trouble from me; I am sorry only the boy I love must die; we die together."

He turned again to the image in the water, seeing it blur through tears, and the vision fading, and as he saw it vanish, he called after: "Where are you going? Stay: do not desert me, I love you so. I cannot touch you; let me keep looking at you always, and in looking nourish my wretched passion!" In his grief he tore his garment from the upper margin, beat his bare breast with hands as pale as marble, and the breast took on a glow, a rosy color, as apples are white and red, sometimes, or grapes can be both green and purple. The water clears, he sees it all once more, and cannot bear it. As yellow wax dissolves with warmth around it, as the white frost is gone in the morning sunshine, Narcissus, in the hidden fire of passion, wanes slowly, with the ruddy color going, the strength and hardihood and comeliness, fading away, and even the very body Echo had loved. She was sorry for him now, though angry still, remembering; you could hear her answer "Alas!" in pity, when Narcissus cried out "Alas!" You could hear her own hands beating her breast when he beat his. "Farewell, dear boy, beloved in vain!" were his last words, and Echo called the same words to him. His weary head sank to the greensward, and death closed the eyes that once had marveled at their owner's beauty.

And even in Hell he found a pool to gaze in, watching his image in the Stygian water. While in the world above, his Naiad sisters mourned him, and Dryads wept for him, and Echo mourned as they did, and wept with them, preparing the funeral pile, the bier, the brandished torches, but when they sought the body, they found nothing, only a flower with a yellow center surrounded with white petals.

The Story of Ganymede, a Very Brief One

The king of the gods once loved a Trojan boy named Ganymede; for once, there was something found that Jove would rather have been than what he was. He made himself an eagle, the only bird able to bear his thunderbolts, went flying on his false wings, and carried off the youngster who now, though much against the will of Juno, tends to the cups of Jove and serves his nectar.

The Story of Apollo and Hyacinthus

There was another boy, who might have had a place in Heaven, at Apollo's order, had fate seen fit to give him time, and still he is, in his own fashion, an immortal. Whenever spring drives winter away, and the Ram succeeds the wintry Fish,[2] he springs to blossom on the green turf. My father[3] loved him dearly, this Hyacinthus, and left Delphi for him, outward from the world's center, on to Sparta, the town that has no walls, and Eurotas River. Quiver and lyre were nothing to him there, no more than his own dignity; he carried the nets for fellows hunting, and held the dogs in leash for them, and with them roamed the trails of the rough mountain ridges. In their train he fed the fire with long association.

It was noon one day; Apollo [and] Hyacinth stripped, rubbed themselves with oil, and tried their skill at discus throwing. Apollo sent the missile far through the air, so far it pierced the clouds, a long time coming down, and when it fell proved both his strength and skill, and Hyacinthus, all eager of his turn, heedless of danger, went running to pick it up, before it settled fully to earth. It bounded once and struck him full in the face, and he grew deadly pale as the pale god caught up the huddled body, trying to warm the dreadful chill that held it, trying to staunch the wound, to hold the spirit with healing herbs, but all the arts were useless. The wound was past all cure. So, in a garden, if one breaks off a violet or poppy or lilies, bristling with their yellow stamen, and they droop to earth, and cannot raise their head, but look on earth, so sank the dying features, the neck, all strength gone, lolled on the shoulder.

"Fallen before your time, O Hyacinthus," Apollo cried, "I see your wound, my crime: you are my sorrow, my reproach; my hand has been your murderer. But how am I to blame? Where is my guilt, except in playing with you, in loving you? I cannot die for you, or with you, either; the law of Fate keeps us apart; it shall not! You will be with me forever, and my songs and music will tell of you, and you will be reborn as a new flower, whose markings will spell out my cries of grief, and there will come a time when a great hero's name will be the same as this flower's markings."

So Apollo spoke, and it was truth he told, for on the ground the blood was blood no longer; in its place a flower grew, brighter than any crimson, like lilies with their silver changed to crimson. That was not all; Apollo kept the promise about the markings and inscribed the flower with his own grieving words: *Ai, Ai* the petals say, Greek for *Alas!* In Sparta, even to this day, they hold their son in honor, and when the day comes round, they celebrate the rites for Hyacinthus, as did their fathers.

The Story of Orpheus and Eurydice

Hymen[4]...took his way to the Ciconian country, where the voice of Orpheus called him, all in vain. He came there, true, but brought with him no auspicious words, no joyful faces, lucky omens…bad as the omens were, the end was worse, for as the bride [Eurydice] went walking across the lawn, a serpent bit her ankle, and she was gone. Orpheus mourned her to the upper world, and then, lest he should leave the shades untried, dared to descend to Styx, passing the portal men call Taenarian….[There, Orpheus tried and failed to bring Eurydice once more to the world of the living.] The double death stunned Orpheus, like the man who turned to rock at sight of Cerberus….At last, complaining the gods of Hell were cruel, he wandered on to Rhodope and Haemus, swept by the north wind, where, for three years, he lived without a woman either because marriage had meant misfortune or he had made a promise. But many women wanted this poet for their own, and many grieved over their rejection. His love was given to young boys only, and he told the Thracians that was the better way: *Enjoy that springtime, take those first flowers!*

…There was a hill, and on it a wide-extending plain, all green, but lacking the darker green of shade, and eger cam there and ran his fingers over the strings, the shade came there to listen. The oak tree came, and many poplar, and the gentle lindens, the beech, the virgin laurel, and the hazel easily …the bare-trunked pine with spreading leafy crest, dear to the mother of the gods since Attis put off his human shape, took on that likeness, and the cone-shaped cypress joined them, now a tree, but once a boy, loved by the god Apollo master of lyre and bow-string, both together.

---

1 For an example of post-Christian homophobic literary distortion, compare these selections to Thomas Bulfinch's translation in the Appendices, below.

2 The zodiacal constellations Ares and Pisces, respectively.

3 Ovid refers to Apollo, the inspiration of many poets, as his "father".

4 The Greek god of marriage.

Kama Sutra

The classic Eastern text of human sexuality is the Indian Kama Sutra. The original composition of the Kama Sutra is attributed to Nandi, the companion of the god Shiva. Shvetaketu, the son of Uddalaka, attempted to summarize these voluminous writings sometime in the eighth century, BCE. Later another man, Babhru, condensed these ideas further. Between the fifth and third centuries before the common era, several more authors took up the writings, making their own additions and subtractions. The Kama Sutra that we know today is not an original work, but an evolved and convoluted compilation of both texts and commentary.

As is customary in all Hindu technical works, including the dictionary, scientific treatises, and such, the Kama Sutra is written in a series of short, condensed verses, called a sutra. These are meant to be memorized, together with the explanations of teachers. The commentaries are an integral part of each sutra.

The texts are arranged in chapter and verse, much like the Judeo-Christian Bible. In those rare cases when the commentary is completely redundant, I have omitted it altogether, indicating the deletion with ellipses.

The following deals with gays, lesbians, and women who perform oral sex. As with all other aspects of human sexuality, practicality dominates the presentation of these concepts. One interesting footnote indicates that, since the importation of Moslem values into Indian culture, the practice of anal intercourse is greatly favored over that of oral sex.

from *The Kama Sutra*

The four previous chapters dealt with women, ranging from the various kinds of embraces to virile behavior.

The fifth chapter, dealing with buccal coition, describes the third sex, which has two aspects.

1   People of the third sex are of two kinds, according to whether their appearance is masculine or feminine.

The third sex is also termed neuter. Those with a feminine appearance have breasts, while those with a masculine appearance have moustaches, body hair, etc. Buccal coition as practiced by both kinds is a part of their nature.

Prostitutes belonging to the third sex are called catamites. The first kind is described as follows:

2   Those with a feminine appearance show it by their dress, speech, laughter, behavior, gentleness, lack of courage, silliness, patience and modesty.

To give themselves a female appearance and imitate their behavior, they arrange their hair in female fashion and imitate their way of talking, etc.

3   They perform the act that takes place between the thighs in their mouth, which is why it is called superior coition.

This term comes down to us from ancient authors.

4   They earn their living from those that seek this form of eroticism.

5   Those who dress as women are taken for prostitutes.

Like prostitutes, they make themselves available to libidinous men, and experience an orgasm, or satisfaction.

The question of transvestites ends here.

6   Those who like men but dissimulate the fact maintain a manly appearance and earn their living as hairdressers or masseurs.

They too practice oral coition, but their sexual desires are dissimulated. Since they look masculine, a man does not immediately reach his goal with them. They practise the profession of masseur, and officially earn their living by massaging limbs.

Since no trust exists to start with, how do they go about getting to erotic action?…

34   Opinions differ on the matter of purity between the authority of the moral codes, occasional local customs, and one's own feelings. One should therefore behave according to one's inclinations.

Moralists condemn the relations of citizens of the eastern country with barbers. Their opposition is a matter of points of view. Moral codes are not revealed texts, but traditions to be consulted. This is why the phrase "according to circumstances" is used....

Having considered buccal coition normal among women, as something which can be practised by women, he again takes up the question of boys.

35   Sometimes, young servants, wearing bright rings in their ears, practice buccal coition with other men.

It is a question of a member of the household, carefully dressed, wearing glittering earrings, a young manservant, working when it pleases him, skillful in his work, pleasing to the eye. He is defined as, "beardless, who can be trusted for acts involving the mouth, wearing jewels, not disfigured by moustaches." Some of these boys, lacking enthusiasm when they get older, turn to women.

36   There are also citizens, sometimes greatly attached to each other and with complete faith in one another, who get married together.

Citizens with this kind of inclination, who renounce women and can do without them willingly because they love each other, get married together, bound by a deep and trusting friendship.

"Do this to me, and afterward I will do it to you." Arranging their bodies in a contrary position, they are indifferent to everything in their moments of passion. They are of two kinds, according to whether they live together openly and without complexes, or dissimulate....

45   For some men, in some countries, in given circumstances or moments, this kind of sexual relationship is not without its own raison d'etre.

Anxiety over matters such as purity or impurity have no meaning in countries like Lata or Sindhu, where buccal coition between men or with women who make a business of it is allowed as freely as kissing on the mouth.

...Although having deep respect for the texts, a man first considers his own interest to decide whether he can practice one form of intercourse or another. In this field, neither man, woman, nor the third sex know any rule.

In this connection:

46   Practiced according to his fantasy and in secret, who can know who, when, how, and why he does it?

...The practice of fellation is common among the hijras, or male prostitutes. This practice, often considered not very refined, is not forbidden by moral texts. It is common even among civilized people, although it is not highly recommended. People with perverse inclinations are attracted by this kind of amusement.

Philostratus

(170-245 CE)

The Letters of Flavius Philostratus (c. 217 CE), were composed in Athens, and doubtless show the influence of the Roman Empire, which by the first century had completely engulfed the Greek city-states. Written in the years following the reign of Hadrian and Antinuous, the letters are a treasure trove of references to gay attitudes, aesthetics, and writings of the past, many now lost to us forever. But mostly, they reveal the mind of a man keenly aware of the charms of a beautiful lad. Many of these letters are imitations of classical models, and many were also used as models by later generations of writers, much in the way that modern song writers use styles and forms of other writers.

Each love letter is addressed, simply, "To a Boy".

from *Love Letters:*

56:     I closed my eyes against you. How against you? I will explain: like men besieged, who close their gates. And you have slipped past the guard and are inside. Tell who brought you in—unless it be that the eyes are a sort of erotic force which has descended upon the soul; and that formerly the soul pondered only such subjects as it wished, and it was engrossed in the most sublime speculations, and its desire was to behold the broad expanses of heaven and to pry into the genuine existence there and to inquire what were the revolutions of the universe and what was the Necessity that drove all this, and it seemed to be an agreeable inquiry—to follow the course of the sun, to share the moon's danger when it waned and its joy when it waxed, to wander in company with the rest of the troop of stars, and not to leave untrodden or unviewed any of the mysteries above the earth; whereas ever since it began to consort with human love and was caught by the eyes of beauty it has ceased to trouble itself about all these other things and has studied just this one thing, and all that it has taken to itself of the outward form it stores within and treasures in its memory, and whatsoever gains entrance is a light by day, and by night becomes a dream.[1]

57:      You are persuaded, I fancy, but you hesitate for fear the deed might bring disgrace. Are you, then, shrinking an act that makes a friend? Was it not because of this that the poems of Homer were filled with beautiful lads when he brought Nireus and Akhilleus to Troy? Was it not because of this that Aristogeiton and Harmodius were friends even to the point of death by the sword? And was it not because of this that Apollo fell into subjection to Admetus and to Branchus? And did not Zeus carry off Ganymede, in whom he delights even more than in his nectar? For you handsome lads, and you alone, inhabit even heaven as your city. Do not begrudge yourself a lover who cannot indeed give you immortality but can give you his own life. If you do not believe me, I am ready to die, if that is your command, at this very moment. If I plait the noose, you inhuman boy, will you not take it from me?

58:      I commend you for cheating time and shaving your cheeks. The smooth skin which left you by nature's law is now restored by art.... So then, with drugs or keen razors or with finger tips or with detergents and herbs or by any means whatsoever, make your beauty longer-lasting. If you do this, you will be imitating the always youthful gods.

64:      The virtue of which you are so proud I know not what to call, whether savage opposition to the dictates of nature or philosophy fortified by boorishness or stubborn timidity towards pleasures or disdainful contempt of life's delights. But whatever it is and whatever the professors may think it, yet, while in repute it is noble, in practise it is rather inhuman. Pray, what greatness is there in being, before you depart from life, a chaste corpse? Garland yourself with flowers before you wither away; anoint yourself with sweet oil before corruption sets in; and make friends before you find yourself solitary. 'Tis well to anticipate at night that other night; to drink before thirsting; to eat before hungering. What day think you is yours? Yesterday? 'Tis dead. Today? It is not yours.[2] Tomorrow? I know not whether you will live to see it. Both you and your days are playthings of fate.

1 Compare this downward spiral of attention, from astronomy down to admiration of a boy, to Socrates' admonition that one should proceed from carnal love to philosophy.

2 Because the youth does not take advantage of it.

William Shakespeare

(1564-1616 CE)

Over the centuries, William Shakespeare's love songs to a younger man have aroused much speculation and debate regarding the bard's sexuality. The debate is complicated by the unfortunate fact that, although Shakespeare is one of the best-known writers in the world, relatively little is known about the man's personal life. We know that Shakespeare was married, and that he was a father; we also are aware that the theatre, in his time as in ours, welcomes and shelters minority sexual expressions.

In his introduction to the Sonnets of Shakespeare, A. L. Rowse argues that the emotions which infuse these Sonnets to his patron, the young and very attractive Lord Southampton, are expressed "in terms of affection, gratitude, and love; though Shakespeare makes it perfectly clear that he has no sexual interest in the youth…" [1] During Shakespeare's relationship with his young patron, however, a love triangle developed between the two men and a certain notorious lady, and the bard found himself writing sonnets double time: some Shakespeare wrote to the young man, some the poet gave to the woman, and some were commissioned by Southampton, who then read them to the lady. As the poems themselves reflect (See Sonnet 36 and following, below), this situation created more than a little stress for all concerned. Also, during this time, the public theatres were closed due to an outbreak of the Plague: for several years Shakespeare was dependent on Southampton for his very survival.

To further complicate matters, for a brief time the poet Christopher Marlowe also entered the picture, making an amorous play for Shakespeare's patron, Southampton. When confronted with the loss of the young man, Shakespeare declares his love boldly and gracefully.

Ultimately, the details of these relationships are irrelevant: a love poem is a love poem is a love poem. In the wider context of men loving men, Shakespeare's Sonnets to Southampton stand as great gay love songs.

from the *Sonnets of Shakespeare*

19

Devouring Time, blunt thou the lion's paws,
And make the earth devour her own sweet brood;
Pluck the keen teeth from the fierce tiger's jaw,
And burn the long-lived phoenix in her blood;
Make glad and sorry seasons as thou fleets,
And do whatever thou wilt, swift-footed Time,
To the wide world and all her fading sweets;
But I forbid thee one most heinous crime;
O, carve not with thy hours my love's fair brow,
Nor draw no lines there with thy antique pen;
Him in his course untainted do allow
For beauty's pattern to succeeding men.
      Yet, do thy worst, old Time: despite thy wrong,
      My love shall ever in my verse live young.

20

A woman's face with Nature's own hand painted
Hast thou, the master-mistress of my passion;
A woman's gentle heart but not acquainted
With shifting change, as is a false woman's fashion;
An eye more bright than theirs, less false in rolling,
Gilding the object whereupon it gazeth;
A man in hue all 'hues' in his controlling,
Which steals men's eyes and women's souls amazeth.
And for a woman wert thou first created;
Till Nature, as she wrought thee, fell a-doting,
And by addition me of thee defeated,
By adding one thing to my purpose nothing.
      But since she prick'd thee out for women's pleasure,
      Mine be thy love and thy love's use their treasure.

26

Lord of my love, to whom in vassalage
Thy merit hath my duty strongly knit,
To thee I send this written embassage,
To witness duty, not to show my wit:
Duty so great, which wit so poor as mine
May make seem bare, in wanting words to show it,
But that I hope some good conceit of thine
In my soul's thought, all naked, will bestow it;
Till whatsoever star that guides me moving
Points on me graciously with fair aspect
And puts apparel on my tattered loving,
To show me worthy of thy sweet respect:
       Then may I dare to boast how I do love thee;
       Till then not show my head where thou mayst prove
me.

29

When, in disgrace with fortune and men's eyes,
I all alone beweep my outcast state
And trouble deaf heaven with my bootless cries
And look upon myself and curse my fate,
Wishing me like to one more rich in hope,
Featured like him, like him with friends possess'd,
Desiring this man's art and that man's scope,
With what I most enjoy contented least;
Yet in these thoughts myself almost despising,
Haply, I think on thee, and then my state,
Like to the lark at break of day arising
From sullen earth sings songs at heaven's gate;
       For thy sweet love remember'd such wealth brings,
       That then I scorn to change my state with kings.

36

Let me confess that we two must be twain,
Although our undivided loves are one:

So shall those blots that do with me remain
Without thy help by me be borne alone.
In our two loves there is but one respect,
Though in our lives a separable spite,
Which though it alter not love's soul effect,
Yet doth it steal sweet hours from my love's delight.
I may not evermore acknowledge thee,
Lest my bewailed guilt should do thee shame,
Nor thou with public kindness honor me,
Unless thou take that honor from my name;
       But do not so; I love thee in such sort
       As, thou being mine, mine is thy good report.

41

Those petty wrongs that liberty commits,
When I am sometime absent from thy heart,
Thy beauty and thy years full well befits,
For still temptation follows where thou art.
Gentle thou art and therefore to be won,
Beauteous thou art, therefore to be assailed;
And when a woman woos, what woman's son
Will sourly leave her till she has prevailed?
Ay me! But thou mightest my seat forbear,
And chide thy beauty and thy straying youth,
Who lead thee in thy riot even there
Where thou art forced to break a two-fold truth,
       Hers, by thy beauty tempting her to thee,
       Thine, by thy beauty being false to me.

42

That thou hast her, it is not all my grief,
And yet it may be said I loved her dearly;
That she hath thee is of my wailing chief,
A loss in love that touches me more nearly.
Loving offenders, thus I will excuse ye:

Thou dost love her, because thou know'st I love her;
And for my sake e'en so doth she abuse me,
Suffering my friend for my sake to approve her.
If I lose thee, my loss is my love's gain,
And losing her, my friend hath found that loss;
Both find each other, I lose both twain,
And both for my sake lay on me this cross:
  But here's the joy; my friend and I are one;
  Sweet flattery! then she loves but me alone.

78

I never saw that you did painting need
And therefore to your fair no painting set;
I found, or thought I found, you did exceed
The barren tender of a poet's debt;
And therefore have I slept in your report,
That you yourself being extant well might show
How far a modern quill doth come too short,
Speaking of worth, what worth in you doth grow.
This silence for my sin you did impute,
Which shall be most my glory, being dumb;
For I impair not beauty being mute,
When others would give life and bring a tomb.
  There lives more life in one of your fair eyes
  Than both[2] your poets can in praise devise.

86

Was it the proud full sail of his great verse[3]
Bound for the prize of all too precious you
That did my ripe thoughts in my brain inhearse
Making their tomb the womb wherein they grew?
Was it his spirit, by spirits taught to write
Above a mortal pitch, that struck me dead?
No, neither he nor his compeers by night
Giving him aid, my verse astonished.

He, nor that affable familiar ghost
Which nightly gulls him with intelligence,
As victors of my silence cannot boast;
I was not sick from any fear of thence:
>   But when your countenance filled up his line,[4]
>   Then lack'd I matter; that enfeebled mine.

1 Rowse, p. 1492-5

2 Shakespeare and Marlowe.

3 Shakespeare refers to Christopher Marlowe.

4 Marlowe's portrait of Leander (see *Hero and Leander* below) is based on Lord Southampton, as is Shakespeare's Adonis in *Venus and Adonis*. Marlowe's sudden and violent death ended the poetic tournament for the favors of Lord Southampton.

Plato

Like his other dialogues, Plato's *Symposium on Love* functions beautifully both as literature and as philosophical discourse.

I have divided the text into two parts, as it seems to me that the semi-serious philosophical discussion in praise of love featured at the beginning of the *Symposium* degenerates completely into riotous drinking and fun at the moment when Alcibiades bursts in on the party. The remainder of the dialogue is a long and very funny complaint on the part of Alcibiades, regarding that young man's failed attempts to seduce Socrates.

from *The Symposium on Love*

A little while afterwards they heard the voice of Alcibiades resounding in the court; he was in a state of great intoxication....

"Hail, friends," he said, appearing at the door crowned with a massive garland of ivy and violets, his head flowing with ribbons. "Will you have a very drunken man as a companion of your revels? Or shall I crown Agathon, which was my purpose in coming, and go away? For I was unable to come yesterday, and therefore I am here today....Will you drink with me or not?"

The company were vociferous in begging that he should take his place among them, and Agathon especially invited him. Thereupon he was led in by the people that were with him; and as he was being led, intending to crown Agathon, he took the ribbons from his own head and held them before his eyes, and thus he was prevented from seeing Socrates, who made way for him, and Alcibiades took the vacant place between Agathon and Socrates, and in taking the place he embraced Agathon and crowned him.

"Take off his sandals," said Agathon, "and let him make a third on the same couch."

"By all means; but who makes the third partner in our

revels?" said Alcibiades, turning round and starting up as he caught sight of Socrates. "By Hercules," he said, "what is this? Here is Socrates always lying in wait for me, and always, as his way is, coming out at all sorts of places; and now, what have you to say for yourself, and why are you lying here, where I perceive that you have contrived to find a place, not by a joker or lover of jokes, like Aristophanes, but by the fairest of the company?"

Socrates turned to Agathon and said, "I must ask you to protect me, Agathon; for the passion of this man has grown quite a serious matter to me. Since I became his admirer I have never been allowed to speak to any other fair one, or so much as to look at them. If I do, he goes wild with envy and jealousy, and not only abuses me, but can hardly keep his hands off me, and at this moment he may do me some harm. Please to see to this; and either reconcile me to him, or, if he attempts violence, protect me, as I am in bodily fear of his mad and passionate attempts."

"There can be no reconciliation between you and me," said Alcibiades; "but for the present I will defer your chastisement. And I must beg you, Agathon, to give me back some of the ribbons that I may crown the marvelous head of this universal despot—I would not have him complain of me for crowning you, and neglecting him—who in conversation is the conqueror of all mankind; and this not only once, as you were the day before yesterday, but always." Whereupon, taking some of the ribbons, he crowned Socrates, and again reclined.

Then he said, "You seem, friends, to be sober, which is a thing not to be endured; you must drink—for that was the agreement under which I was admitted—and I elect myself master of the feast until you are well drunk. Let us have a large goblet, Agathon..."

Eryximachus said, "What is this, Alcibiades? Are we to have neither conversation nor singing over our cups, but simply to drink as if we were thirsty?...Before you appeared we had passed a resolution that each of us in turn should make a speech in praise of love..."

"That is good, Eryximachus," said Alcibiades, "and yet the comparison of a drunken man's speech with those of sober men is hardly fair; and I would like to know, sweet friend, whether you really believe what Socrates was just now saying; for I can assure you that the very reverse is the fact, and that if I praise anyone but himself in his presence, whether god or man, he will hardly keep his hands off me."

"For shame," said Socrates.

"Hold your tongue," said Alcibiades, "for, by Poseidon, there is no one else whom I will praise, when you are of the company."

"Well then," said Eryximachus, "if you like, praise Socrates."

"What do you think, Eryximachus?" said Alcibiades. "Shall I attack him and inflict the punishment before you all?"

"What are you about?" said Socrates; "are you going to raise a laugh at my expense? Is that the meaning of your praise?"

"I am going to speak the truth, if you will permit me."

"I not only permit, but exhort you to speak the truth."…

"See how fond [Socrates] is of the fair? He is always with them and is always being smitten by them, and then again he knows nothing and is ignorant of all such things—such is the appearance that he puts on. Is he not like a Silenus[1] in this? To be sure he is: his outer mask is the carved mask of Silenus; but, O my companions in drink, when he is opened, what temperance there is residing within! Know you that beauty and wealth and honor, at which the many wonder, is of no account with him, and are utterly despised by him: he regards not at all the people who are gifted with them; mankind is nothing to him; all his life is spent in mocking and flouting at them. But when I opened him, and looked within at his serious purpose, I saw in him divine and golden images of such fascinating beauty that I was ready at that moment to do whatever Socrates commanded: they may have escaped the observation of others, but I saw them.

"Now I fancied that he was seriously enamored of my beauty, and I thought that I should therefore have a grand opportunity of hearing him tell what he knew, for I had a wonderful opinion of the attractions of my youth. In the prosecution of this design, when I next went to see him, I sent away the attendant who usually accompanied me (I will confess the whole truth, and beg you to listen; and if I speak falsely, do you, Socrates, expose the falsehood.) Well, he and I were alone together, and I thought that when there was nobody with us, I should hear him speak the language which lovers use to their loves when they are by themselves, and I was delighted. Nothing of the sort; he conversed as usual, and spent the day with me and then went away.

"Afterwards I challenged him to the palaestra;[2] and he wrestled with me and closed with me several times when there was no one present; I fancied that I might succeed in this manner. Not a bit; I made no way with him. Lastly, as I had failed hitherto, I thought that I must take stronger measures and attack him boldly, and, as I had begun, not give him up, but see how matters stood between him and me.

"So I invited him to sup with me, just as if he were a fair youth, and I a designing lover. He was not easily persuaded to come; he did however after a while accept the invitation, and when he came the first time, he wanted to go away at once as soon as supper was over, and I had not the face to detain him. The second time, still in pursuance of my design, after we had supped, I went on conversing far into the night, and when he wanted to go away, I pretended that the hour was late and that he had much better remain. So he lay on the couch next to me, the same on which we had supped, and there was no one but ourselves sleeping in the apartment. All this may be told without shame to anyone. But what follows I could hardly tell you if I were sober. Yet as the proverb says, *'in vino veritas'*, whether with boys or without them; and therefore I must speak. Nor, again, should I be justified in concealing the lofty actions of Socrates when I come to praise him. Moreover, I have felt the serpent's sting; and he who has suffered, as they say, is willing to tell his fellow sufferers only, as they alone will be likely to understand him and will not be extreme in judging the sayings or the doings which are wrung from his agony. For I have been bitten by more than a viper's tooth; I have known in my soul, or in my heart, or in some other part, that worst of pangs, more violent in ingenuous youth than any a serpent's tooth, the pang of philosophy, which will make a man do or say anything. And you whom I see here around me, Phaedrus and Agathon and Eryximachus and Pausanias and Aristomedus and Aristophanes, all of you, and I need not say Socrates himself, have had experience of the same madness and passion in your longings after wisdom. Therefore listen and excuse my doings and sayings now. But let the attendants and other profane and unmannered persons close the doors of their ears.

"When the lamp was put out and the servants had gone away, I thought that I must be plain with him and have no more ambiguity. So I gave him a shake and I said: 'Socrates, are you asleep?'

"'No,' he said.

"'Do you know what I am meditating?'

"'What are you meditating?' he said.

"'I think', I replied, 'that of all the lovers whom I have ever had you are the only one who is worthy of me, and you appear to be too modest to speak. Now I feel that I should be a fool to refuse you this or any other favor, and therefore I come to lay at your feet all that I have and all that my friends have, in the hope that you will assist me in the way of virtue, which I desire above all things, and in which I believe that you can help me better than anyone else. And I should certainly have more reason to be ashamed of what wise men say if I were to refuse a favor to such as you, than of what the world, who are mostly fools, would say of me if I granted it.'

"To these words he replied in the ironical manner which is so characteristic of him: 'Alcibiades, my friend, you have indeed an elevated aim if what you say is true, and if there really is in me any power by which you may become better; truly you must see in me some rare beauty infinitely higher than any which I see in you. And therefore, if you mean to share with me and to exchange beauty for beauty, you will have greatly the advantage of me; you will gain true beauty in exchange for appearance—like Diomed, gold in exchange for brass.[3] But look again, sweet friend, and see whether you are not deceived in me. The mind begins to grow critical when the bodily eye fails, and it will be a long time before you get old.'

"Hearing this I said: 'I have told you my purpose, which is quite serious, and do you consider what you think best for you and me.'

"'That is good,' he said; 'at some other time then we will consider and act as seems best about this and about other matters.' Whereupon I fancied that he was smitten, and that the words which I had uttered like arrows had wounded him, and so without waiting to hear more I got up, and throwing my coat about me crept under his threadbare cloak, as the time of the year was winter, and there I lay the whole night long having this wonderful monster in my arms. This again, Socrates, will not be denied by you. And yet, notwithstanding all, he was so superior to my solicitations, so contemptuous and derisive and disdainful of my beauty, which really, as I fancied, had some attractions—hear, O judges; for judges you shall be of the haughty virtue of Socrates—nothing more happened, but in the morning when I awoke (let all the gods and goddesses be my witnesses) I arose as from the couch of a father or an elder brother.

"What do you suppose must have been my feelings, after this rejection, at the thought of my own dishonor? And yet I could not help wondering at his natural temperance and self-restraint and manliness. I never imagined that I could have met with a man such as he is in wisdom and endurance. And therefore I could not be angry with him or renounce his company, any more than I could hope to win him....and my only chance of captivating him by my personal attractions had failed. So I was at my wit's end; no one was ever more hopelessly enslaved by another....

"This, friends is my praise of Socrates. I have added my blame of him for his ill treatment of me; and he has ill treated not only me, but Charmides the son of Glaucon, and Euthydemus the son of Diocles, and many others in the same way—beginning as their lover he has ended by making them pay their addresses to him.

"Wherefore I say to you, Agathon: Be not deceived by

him; learn from me and take warning, and do not be a fool and learn by experience, as the proverb says."

When Alcibiades had finished, there was a laugh at his outspokenness; for he seemed to be still in love with Socrates.

"You are sober, Alcibiades, or you should never have gone so far about to hide the purpose of your satyr's praises, for all this long story is only an ingenious circumlocution, of which the point comes in by way at the end; you want to get up a quarrel between me and Agathon, and your notion is that I ought to love you and nobody else, and that you and you only ought to love Agathon. But the plot of this satiric or Selenic drama has been detected, and you must not allow him, Agathon, to set us at variance."

"I believe you are right," said Agathon, "and I am disposed to think that his intention in placing himself between you and me was only to divide us; but he shall gain nothing by that move; for I will go and lie on the couch next to you."

"Yes, yes," replied Socrates, "by all means come and lie on the couch below me."[4]

"Alas," said Alcibiades, "how I am fooled by this man; he is determined to get the better of me at every turn. I do beseech you, allow Agathon to lie between us."

Certainly not," said Socrates, "as you praised me, and I in turn ought to praise my neighbor on the right, he will be out of order in praising me again when he ought rather to be praised by me, and I must entreat you to consent to this, and not be jealous, for I have a great desire to praise the youth."

"Hurrah!" cried Agathon. "I will rise instantly, that I may be praised by Socrates."

"The usual way," said Alcibiades; "where Socrates is, no one else has a chance with the fair; and how readily has he invented a specious reason for attracting Agathon to himself."

Agathon rose that he might take his place on the couch by Socrates, when suddenly a band of revelers entered, and spoiled the order of the banquet...and everyone was compelled to drink large quantities of wine....

Then, when the day was already dawning... Socrates...rose to depart; Aristomedus, as his manner was, followed him. At the Lyceum he took a bath, and passed the day as usual. In the evening he retired to rest at his own house.

1 Alcibiades here refers to a sort of carved mask, filled inside with tiny statues of gods and instruments.

2 Training school for wrestling and other athletic sports.

3 Iliad, VI, 234-236.

4 At Greek all-male dinners, such as the one from which this Symposium is detailed, "Men and adolescents reclined on the same couch, the younger one in front, next to the table. The man made him drink, caressed him and made him, if I may say so, his mistress." (A. J. Festugière, Etudes de religion grecque et hellénistique, quoted by Daniélou, in Shiva and Dionysus, p. 151)

David and Jonathan
(c. 1000 BCE)

The great gay love story of the Bible is the saga of David and Jonathan. The books of First and Second Samuel[1] in the Christian Bible detail the rise and fall of the first king of the Israelites, Saul, and the subsequent rise to power of David (c. 1000 BCE); linking these two kings, between whom deadly enmity arises after initial love, is their mutual love for the king's son, prince Jonathan.[2]

It is quite likely that David was still in his teens when he first came to the royal court, and reports indicate that he was very attractive. The anonymous writers of the books of Samuel describe David as having "a ruddy complexion and beautiful eyes", and "ruddy and comely in appearance". It is this David that we should keep in mind when we read the following story, for it is this beautiful lad that King Saul loves, and to whom Prince Jonathan pledges eternal love and devotion.[3]

Since the well-chronicled escapades of King David's reign suggest rampant heterosexuality, why should we assume that he indulged in gay sexual relationships as a youth? In answering this, we must keep in mind that institutional pederasty was common in the ancient world, especially as a method of indoctrination into exclusive communities. Likewise, common sense tells us that David is not the first beautiful young man to have caught the eye of a king, nor is he the first to have used sex as a means of career advancement. To people who insist that David was not gay, I offer the theory that Jonathan was in love, and David was smart.

To shorten the (rather long) narrative, I have paraphrased extraneous passages; to avoid a forest of quotation marks, my own editorial condensations appear in brackets.

from *The Revised Standard Version of the Bible*

[The tall and handsome Saul[4] has become king following a series of amazing political and military successes. Despite initial favor with the Israeli god, Yahweh, and extraordinary popularity among the Israelis, the king is tormented by an "evil spirit from the LORD".[5] Saul's men suggest that soothing music might drive the evil spirit away, and one of the men recalls a young shepherd boy named David[6] who plays beautiful music on his lyre. Saul accordingly]

sent messengers to Jesse, and said, "Send me David your son, who is with the sheep."
...And David came to Saul, and entered his service. And Saul loved him greatly; and David became his armor bearer.
And Saul sent to Jesse, saying, "Let David remain in my service, for he has found favor in my sight."
And whenever the evil spirit from God came upon Saul, David took the lyre and played it with his hand; so Saul was refreshed, and was well, and the evil spirit departed from him....
Now David was the son of...Jesse, who had eight sons. The three eldest sons of Jesse had followed Saul to the battle...but David went back and forth from Saul to feed his father's sheep at Bethlehem....[7]

[In their war against the Philistines, the Israelites are continuously daunted by Goliath; for forty days, the giant dares any Israeli to meet him in single combat. Each day the challenge is unanswered, and military morale plummets. Finally, David slays Goliath with his sling, and the Israelites rout the Philistines in a tremendous battle.]

And the Israelites came back from chasing the Philistines, and they plundered their camp. And David took the head of [Goliath] and brought it to Jerusalem[8]...And as David returned from the slaughter of the Philistine, Abner took him, and brought him before Saul with the head of the Philistine in his hand.
And Saul said to him, "Whose son are you, young man?"[9]
And David answered, "I am the son of your servant Jesse the Bethlehemite."

When he had finished speaking to Saul, the soul of Jonathan was knit to the soul of David, and Jonathan loved him as his own soul. And Saul took him that day, and would not let him return to his father's house. Then Jonathan made a covenant with David, because he loved him as his own soul.[10] And Jonathan stripped himself of the robe that was upon him, and gave it to David, and his armor and even his sword and his bow and his girdle.

And David went out and was successful wherever Saul sent him, so that Saul set him over the men of war....

[Given his own military command while still a youth, David's political star rises rapidly. His enormous success in his campaigns against the Philistines soon eclipses king Saul's military fame. The townspeople, cheering the return of the triumphant army, sing that]

"Saul has slain his thousands, and David his ten thousands."

And Saul was very angry, and this saying displeased him....And on the morrow an evil spirit from God rushed upon Saul, and he raved within his house, while David was playing the lyre, as he did day by day. Saul had his spear in his hand, and Saul cast the spear, for he thought, "I will pin David to the wall." But David evaded him twice.

[Calm is eventually restored, but Saul now begins seeking a way to control David. Initially, he tries to marry David to his eldest daughter; David refuses this offer several times, saying he is unworthy to wed the king's eldest daughter. Saul, learning of his younger daughter Michal's infatuation with the hero, marries her off to David.

Soon Saul's envy of David turns to hatred, and the king makes up his mind to kill youth.]

And Saul spoke to his son Jonathan and all his servants, that they should kill David. But Jonathan, Saul's son, delighted much in David.

And Jonathan told David, "Saul my father seeks to kill you; therefore take heed for yourself in the morning, stay in a secret place and hide yourself; and I will go out and stand beside my father in the field where you are; and if I learn anything I will tell you."

[Jonathan intercedes for David with Saul, reminding the king of how useful the youth has been, and Saul repents, pledging to protect him. David returns to the court, and for a time all is as it was.

But before long, the 'evil spirit from the LORD' again comes upon Saul, and again the king tries to kill David, who escapes and flees for his life.]

Then David… came and said before Jonathan, "What have I done? What is my guilt? And what is my sin before your father, that he seeks my life?"

And he said to him, "Far from it! You shall not die. Behold, my father does nothing, whether great or small, without disclosing it to me; and why should my father hide this from me? It is not so."

But David swore again, "But your father knows well that I have found favor in your eyes; and he thinks, 'Let not Jonathan know this, lest he be grieved.' But truly, as the LORD lives and as your soul lives, there is but a step between me and death."

Then said Jonathan to David, "Whatever you say, I will do for you."

David said to Jonathan, "…[D]eal kindly with your servant, for you have brought your servant into a sacred covenant with you, a covenant of the LORD. But if there is guilt in me, slay me yourself; why should you bring me to your father?"

And Jonathan said, "Far be it from you! If I knew that it was determined by my father that evil come upon you, would I not tell you myself?"

Then David said to Jonathan, "Who will tell me if your father answers you roughly?"

And Jonathan said to David, "Come, let us go out into the field." So they both went out into the field.

And Jonathan said to David, "The LORD, the God of Israel, be witness! When I have sounded my father, about this time tomorrow, or the third day, behold, if he is well disposed toward David, shall I not then send and disclose it to you? But should it please my father to do you harm, the LORD do so to Jonathan and more also, if I do not disclose it to you, and send you away, that you may go in safety. May the LORD be with you, as he has been with my father. If I am still alive, show me the loyal love of the LORD, that I may not die; and do not cut off your loyalty from my house forever. When the LORD has cut off every one of the enemies of David from the face of the earth, let not the name of Jonathan be cut off from the house of David…"

And Jonathan made David swear again by his love for him; for he loved him as he loved his own soul.

Then Jonathan said to him: "…And as for the matter of which you and I have spoken, behold, the LORD is between you and me forever."

[After a few days, Saul realizes that David has eluded him again, and the king immediately guesses Jonathan's part in David's latest escape:]

Then Saul's anger was kindled against Jonathan, and he said to him, "You son of a perverse, rebellious woman,[11] do I not know that you have chosen the son of Jesse to your own shame, and to the shame of your mother's nakedness?[12] For as long as the son of Jesse lives upon the earth, neither you nor your kingdom shall be established. Therefore send and fetch him to me, for he shall surely die."

Then Jonathan answered Saul his father and said, "Why should he be put to death? What has he done?"

But Saul cast his spear at him to smite him; so Jonathan knew that his father was determined to put David to death. And Jonathan rose from the table in fierce anger and ate no food the second day of the month, for he was grieved for David, because his father had disgraced him.

[The next day, Jonathan uses a pre-arranged signal to inform David that his father indeed wishes David dead. As David hides, Jonathan sends his servant back to the city with his bow and arrows. As soon as the boy was gone:]

David rose from behind the stone heap [where he had been hiding] and fell on his face to the ground, and bowed three times; and they kissed one another, and wept with one another, until David exceeded.[13]

Then Jonathan said to David, "Go in peace, for as much as we have sworn both of us in the name of the LORD, saying, 'The LORD shall be between you and me, and between my descendants and your descendants, forever.'"

And [David] rose and departed, and Jonathan went into the city.

[A period of turmoil follows, in which Saul, determined to kill David, hunts the young man and his fleeing retinue in the wilderness. David passes up several chances to kill the king, always escaping from Saul's attempts to kill him. Knowing that Saul will not rest until he is destroyed, David takes his men to the city of Gath. Upon learning of this, Saul decides to pursue the matter no further. David remains in Gath for sixteen months, during which time he and his people conduct several raids against neighboring cities.

In time the Philistines attack the Israelites again, on Mount Gilboa, and overcome them. In this battle, Jonathan and Saul are slain, and their bodies are fastened to the wall of the Philistine city Bethshan. After a while, the men of Jabesh-Gilead come to the town by night, take down the bodies, and cremate them. When proof of this reaches him,]

David took hold of his clothes, and rent them; and so did all the men who were with him; and they mourned for Saul and for his son Jonathan....

And David lamented with this lamentation over Saul and Jonathan his son...

"Thy glory, O Israel, is slain upon thy high places!
How are the mighty fallen!...
Saul and Jonathan, beloved and lovely!

In death and in life they were not divided;
they were swifter than eagles;
they were stronger than lions....
Jonathan lies slain upon thy high places.
I am distressed for you, my brother Jonathan;
very pleasant have you been to me,
your love to me was wonderful,
surpassing the love of women.
How are the mighty fallen,
and the weapons of war perished!"

[David is then anointed by the men of the house of Judah as king. Following his accession to the throne, David seeks for a way to honor his oath[14] to Jonathan:]

"Is there still anyone left of the house of Saul, that I may show him kindness for Jonathan's sake?"
...Ziba said to the king, "There is still a son of Jonathan; he is crippled in his feet."

[The crippled youth is brought before the king, who says:]

"Do not fear; for I will show you kindness for the sake of your father Jonathan, and I will restore to you the lands of Saul your father; and you shall eat at my table always."
...So Mephibosheth ate at David's table like one of the king's sons....

1 In the Jewish cannon, these books are called First and Second Kings.

2 1 Samuel 16, 17

3 The gay sculptor Michaelangelo Buonarrotti (1475-1564 CE) has forever captured the glory of youth in full flower with his colossal sculpture of David, which depicts the young slayer of Goliath poised and ready for battle, sling over his shoulder.

4 "...Kish...had a son whose name was Saul, a handsome young man. There was not a man among the people of Israel more handsome than he; from his shoulders upward he was taller than any of the people...." (1 Samuel 9:1-2)

5 1 Samuel 16:14, 16:23, 17:53, 18:10, etc.

6 Hebrew: beloved

7 Bethlehem, David's village, is located five miles south of Jerusalem.

8 This battle took place at Socoh, some thirty miles south and slightly west of Jerusalem.

9 This apparent lapse in Saul's memory may be the literary result of the overlapping of two different narratives; or, more likely, the formal tone and the asking of seemingly-rhetorical questions may be the result of royal protocol, as Saul here is publicly recognizing David in front of the people.

10 This euphemism for gay love found its way into medieval literature, where it appears, for example, in accounts of Richard the Lion-Hearted's royal love for Philip of France. See Boswell, Christianity... p. 231.

11 Literally, "You son of a bitch!"

12 A stock phrase, found also in Levitical codes governing sexual relationships within a tribe.

13 See Appendix 1, "Biblical Variation on 1 Samuel 20:41" for more on this verse.

14 Boswell and others have compared the oaths of loyalty the two men make to those that heterosexual couples use in wedding ceremonies.

Martial

(First Century CE)

John Boswell observes that, in many important ways, the Greco-Roman culture is the foundation and model of our own; Michael asserts that America is the reincarnation of the ancient Roman Empire. An examination of the values, practices, and ethics of the Romans, as revealed by Martial's deeply incisive wit, throws an interesting light on modern American culture. To read Martial is to experience one of our own cultural ancestors.

An epigram is defined as "a concise poem dealing pointedly and often satirically with a single thought or event and often ending with an ingenious turn of thought."[1] In the first century of the common era, the Roman writer Juvensius Martial refined the epigram into a potent and biting art-form, amusing his public with small volumes containing pithy portraits of people and places in the Empire. More often than not, the names of his subjects were disguised with pseudonyms, themselves often carrying a double meaning.

To observers and critics of the Empire, the great obscenity of Roman life was not the lusty abandon with which sexual experience was pursued, but the hypocrisy of a system under which the citizenry said one thing and did another. An example of this would be the practice of marrying to produce children, usually with solemn vows of fidelity, and then maintaining lovers, of any sex or age, to satisfy one's desires outside of the marriage. Such hypocrites are Martial's favorite targets.

A casual reader might think, after glancing through his *Epigrams,* that Martial detested homosexual behavior. But this is not the case: it is clear from his tender tone when elegizing a gay youth who has died young (VI:68) or when honoring two old gay lovers (I:93) that the object of sexual attraction is irrelevant to Martial: integrity, fidelity, and the quality of behavior are his standards, not the gender of someone's lovers.

from *Epigrams:*

6.	As the eagle bore the boy[2] through the airs of heaven, the timid talons did not harm their clinging freight. Now Caesar's lions are won over by their prey and the hare plays safely in the massive jaws. Which do you think the greater marvel? Behind both stands the Highest. The one is Caesar's, the other Jove's.

24.	Decianus, you see that fellow there with the rough hair, whose beetling brow frightens even you, who talks of Curii and Camilli, freedom's champions? Don't believe his looks. He took a husband yesterday.

31.	These locks, all he has from crown down, does Encolopus, the darling of his master the centurion, vow to you, Phoebus, when Prudens shall attain the rank of Chief Centurion which he wants and deserves. Cut the long tresses as soon as may be, Phoebus, while no down darkens his soft cheeks and flowing locks grace his milk-white neck. And so that master and lad may long enjoy your bounty, make him soon shorn, but late a man.

93.	Aquinus rests by the side of loyal Fabricius, who is glad to have been first to go to the Elysian dwellings. A double altar attests the rank of Chief Centurion; but what you read in the shorter inscription means more: "Both were united in the sacred bond of an honorable life, and, what fame seldom knows, both were friends."

from Book Two:

43.	"Friends must share." Is *this,* is *this* your sharing, Candidus, that you boom about so grandly night and day? A gown washed in Lacedaemonian Galaesus covers you, or one that Parma furnished from a special flock. As for mine, dummy number one[3] that has suffered the horns of a raging bull wouldn't care to be called its owner. The land of Cadmus has sent you an Agenorian cloak; you won't sell my scarlet for three *sesterces*. You balance Libyan tabletops on Indian tusks; my beech wood board is propped up on earthenware. For you outsize mullets cover yellow dishes gold-inlaid; a crab blushes on my plate, red like himself. Your waiters could vie with the Ilian catamite; but my hand comes to *my* assistance in lieu of Ganymede. Out of so much wealth you give nothing to your faithful old crony and you say "friends must share", Candidus?

45.   Your cock, which wouldn't stand up, has been cut, Glyptus. You're out of your mind. What did you want with the knife? You *were* a eunuch.[4]

47.   Gallus, smoother than Cytherea's shells, fly, I warn you, the crafty nets of the notorious adulteress. Do you trust in your buttocks? The husband is no sodomite. There are two things he does: he gives suck or he fucks.

60.   Hyllus my boy, you fuck the wife of an armed tribune, fearing nothing worse than a boyish punishment.[5] Alas and alack, you'll be castrated as you sport. Now you'll say to me: "That's not allowed." Well, how about what you're up to, Hyllus. Is that allowed?

61.   In the springtime of your cheeks when the down was still dubious, your shameless tongue licked male middles. Now that your sorry head has earned the scorn of undertakers and the disgust of a wretched executioner, you use your mouth otherwise; delighted by excess of spite, you bark at whatever name is put to you. Better that your noxious tongue stick in genitals. It was cleaner when it sucked.

62.   You pluck your chest and your shins and your arms, and your shaven cock is ringed with short hairs. This, Labienus, you do for your mistress' sake, as everybody knows. For whose sake, Labienus, do you depilate your ass?

28.   Glaucias, the well-known freedman of Melior, at whose death all Rome wept, the short-lived delight of his affectionate patron, reposes beneath this marble sepulcher close to the Flaminian Way. He was a youth of pure morals, of simple modesty, of ready wit, and of rare beauty. To twice six harvests completed, the youth was just adding another year. Traveler, who laments his fate, may you never have aught else to lament!

29.   Glaucia was not of the lower class of house slaves, nor of such as were sold in the common market: but he was a youth worthy of the tender affections of his master, and, before he could as yet appreciate the kindness of his patron, he was already made the freedman of Melior. This was the reward of his morals and beauty. Who was more attractive than he? or whose face more resembled that of Apollo? Short is the life of those who possess uncommon endowments, and rarely do they reach old age. Whatever you love, pray that you may not love it too much.

33.   You have never seen anything more pitiable, Matho, than sodomite Sabellus, once the happiest of mankind. Thefts, flights, deaths of slaves, fires, bereavements afflict him. Poor soul, he has even taken to fornicating [with women].

36.   So large is your cock, Papylus, and so long your nose, that you can sniff it whenever you erect.

54.   If, Aulus, you forbid Sextilianus to speak of his "so great" and "so great", the poor fellow will be scarce able to put three words together. "What does he mean?" you ask. I will tell you what I suspect: namely, that Sextilianus is fallen in love with his "so great" and "so great".

68.   Naiads, weep for your crime, yes weep all over Lucrine Lake, and let Thetis herself hear your wails! A boy has been snatched to his death in Baiae's waters, Eutychus, your sweet companion, Castricus. He was the partner of your cares, your

beguiling solace, the love, the Alexis of our poet. Did a wanton nymph see you naked under the glassy water[6] and send Hylas back to Alcides [Hercules]? Or does the goddess now neglect womanish Hermaphroditus, stirred to passion by the embrace of a youthful *man?* Be that as it may, whatever the cause of the sudden rape, may both earth, I pray, and water be kind to you.

from Book Twelve:

35.   As though you and I were on terms of total frankness, Callistratus, it's your habit to tell me often that you have been sodomized. You are not so frank as you wish to be thought, Callistratus. For when a man tells such things, there are more things he doesn't tell.

42.   Bearded Callistratus married rugged Afer in the usual form in which a virgin marries a husband. The torches shone in front, the wedding veil covered his face, and you, Thalassus, you did not lack your words. Even the dowry was declared. Are you still not satisfied, Rome? Are you waiting for him to give birth? [7]

64.   A boy more beautiful in face and hair than his rose-cheeked pages Cinna has made a cook. Cinna is a greedy fellow.

85.   You say that sodomites smell at the mouth. If what you say is true, Fabullus, where do you think cunt-lickers smell?

86.   You have thirty boys and as many girls; you have one cock, and it doesn't rise. What will you do?

91.   Since you share a couch and a male concubine with your husband, Magulla, tell me why you don't share a page too. You sigh. There's a reason, you're afraid of the flagon.[8]

97.   Your wife is a girl such as a husband would hardly ask for in his most extravagant prayers, rich, noble, cultivated, virtuous. You burst your loins, Bassus, but you do it with long-

---

haired boys whom you have procured for yourself with your wife's dowry. And your cock, which she bought for many thousands, returns to your lady so languid that, whether excited by coaxing words or requested with a soft thumb, it won't rise. Have some shame, for a change; or let us go to law. It's not yours, Bassus. You sold it.

1 Merriam Webster's New Collegiate Dictionary.

2 Ganymede.

3 The *pila* was a dummy thrown into the ring to enrage the bull at a bull fight; the first dummy would be the worst gored and trampled.

4 Cybele's priests, called Galli ("Gauls", i.e. Galatians), castrated themselves, hence gallus = eunuch. "Glyptus" (carved) presumably had joined the fraternity; see also Paul's epistle to the Galatians, Chapter 5, in the Christian Bible.

5 that is, to be sodomized.

6 These references are to classical myths dealing with drowning.

7 Martial here refers to the Roman taboo (later codified into a seldom-used law; see Boswell "Christianity...") against an adult, bearded male's submission to sodomy. Martial's ire in this epigram is directed not at the lovers for marrying, but at Roman society for hypocritically supporting both the taboo and their marriage.

8 I. e. poison.

Christopher Marlowe

(1564-1593)

One of the most celebrated and notorious poets of Queen Elizabeth's court was the dashing and talented playwright Christopher Marlowe. During his short lifetime, he created a legacy of poetry, plays, and intrigue that would keep historians and gossips alike buzzing for many years. Marlowe scandalized all London when he declared that, "Those that love not boys and tobacco are fools."

Shakespeare and Marlowe, born only two months apart, maintained a professional rivalry throughout their careers, which peaked when the aggressive and gallant Kit Marlowe made an amorous play for the young Lord Southampton, Shakespeare's patron. Marlowe's flattering descriptions of Southampton as Leander in the erotic neoclassical poem *Hero and Leander* apparently succeeded in luring the young man away from Shakespeare, at least for a time.[1]

Christopher Marlowe died in a tavern at the age of twenty-nine, stabbed during a brawl over the bar bill. At the time, many of his works were unfinished; some of these were later finished by George Chapman. Sadly, Marlowe's genius could not safeguard his work from the Christian church: in 1599, Archbishop Whitgift ordered all copies of Marlowe's translations of Ovid's *Elegies* publicly burned.[2]

Before Shakespeare revolutionized the English stage with his comedies, histories and tragedies, Marlowe had transformed the blank verse format into a vehicle for his own powerful style, paving the way for Shakespeare's later success with the idiom. Marlowe's *Doctor Faustus* remains a classic to this day; *The Passionate Shepherd To His Love* is the most often quoted poem in the English language. By contrast, had Shakespeare died at Marlowe's age, it is doubtful that the bard's work would still be known today.

Solely in the interest of clarity, I have regularized the Elizabethan spelling of the following excerpts.

from *The Tragedy of Dido, Queen of Carthage:*

[Here the curtains draw, there is discovered Jupiter dandling
Ganymede upon his knee, and Mercury lying asleep.]

Jupiter: Come gentle Ganymede and play with me,
   I love thee well, say Juno what she will.
Ganymede: I am much better for your worthless love,
   That will not shield me from her shrewish blows:
   Today when, as I filled into your cups,
   And held the cloth of pleasance while you drank,
   She reached me such a rap for that I spilled,
   As made the blood run down about mine ears.
Jupiter: What? She dares strike the darling of my thoughts?
   By Saturn's soul, and this earth threat'ning hair,
   That shaken thrice, makes Natures buildings quake,
   I vow, that if she but once frown on thee more,
   To hang her meteor like twixt heaven and earth,
   And bind her hand and foot with golden cords,
   As once I did for harming Hercules.
Ganymede: Might I see but that pretty sport a foot,
   O how would I with Helen's brother laugh,
   And bring the gods to wonder at the game:
   Sweet Jupiter, if 'ere I pleas'd thine eye,
   Or seemed fair wall'd in with eagle's wings,
   Grace my immortal beauty with this boon,
   And I will spend my time in thy bright arms.
Jupiter: What is't sweet wag I should deny thy youth?
   Whose face reflects such pleasures to mine eyes,
   As I exhal'd with thy fire darting beams,
   Have oft driven back the horses of the night,
   When as they would have held thee from my sight:
   Sit on my knee, and call for thy content,
   Control proud fate, and cut the thread of time.
   Why, are not all the gods at thy command?
   And heaven and earth the bounds of thy delight?
   Vulcan shall dance to make thee laughing sport,

And my nine daughters sing when thou art sad,
From Juno's bird I'll pluck her spotted pride,
To make thee fans wherewith to cool thy face,
And Venus' swans shall shed their silver down,
To sweeten out the slumbers of thy bed:
Hermes no more shall show the world his wings,
If that thy fancies in his feathers dwell,
But as this one I'll tear them all from him,
[plucks a feather from Mercury's wings.]
Do thou but say their color pleaseth me.
Hold here, my little love: these linked gems,
[gives jewels.]
My Juno wore upon her wedding day,
Put thou about thy neck my own sweet heart,
And trick thy arms and shoulders with my theft.
Ganymede: I would have a jewel for mine ear,
And a fine brooch to put in my hat,
And then I'll hug with you a hundred times.
Jupiter: And shall have, Ganymede, if thou wilt be my love.
[Enter Venus.]
Venus: I, this is it, you can sit toying there,
And playing with that female wanton boy,
While my Aeneas wanders on the seas…
False Jupiter, reward'st thou virtue so?
What? is not pity exempt from woe?…
Jupiter: I will take order for that presently…
Venus farewell, thy son shall be our care:
Come, Ganymede, we must about this gear.
[Exeunt Jupiter with Ganymede.]

from *Hero and Leander:*

Amorous Leander, beautiful and young,
(Whose tragedy divine Musaeus sung)
Dwelt at Abydos; since him dwelt there none
For whom succeeding times make greater moan.
His dangling tresses that were never shorn,
Had they been cut and unto Colchas[3] borne,

Would have allured the vent'rous youth of Greece
To hazard more than for the Golden Fleece.
Fair Cynthia wished his arms might be her sphere;
Grief makes her pale, because she moves not there.
His body was as straight as Circe's wand;
Jove might have sipped out nectar from his hand.
Even as delicious meat is to the taste,
So was his neck in touching, and surpassed
The white of Pelops' shoulder. I could tell ye
How smooth his breast was, and how white his belly,
And whose immortal fingers did imprint
That heavenly path, with many a curious dint,
That runs along his back; but my rude pen
Can hardly blazon forth the loves of men,
Much less of powerful gods; let it suffice
That my slack Muse sings of Leander's eyes,
Those orient cheeks and lips, exceeding his
That leapt into the water for a kiss
Of his own shadow, and despising many,
Died ere he could enjoy the love of any.[4]
Had wild Hippolytus[5] Leander seen,
Enamored of his beauty had he been;
His presence made the rudest peasant melt,
That in the vast uplandish country dwelt;
The barbarous Thracian[6] soldier, moved with naught,
Was moved with him, and for his favor sought.
Some swore he was a maid in man's attire,
For in his looks were all that men desire:
A pleasant smiling cheek, a speaking eye,
A brow for love to banquet royally;
And such as knew he was a man would say,
"Leander, thou art made for amorous play;
Why art thou not in love, and loved of all?
Though thou be fair, yet be not thine own thrall."…

…What is it now, but mad Leander dares?
"O Hero, Hero" thus he cried full oft;
And then he got him to a rock aloft,

Where having spied her tower, long time he stared on't
And prayed the narrow toiling Hellespont
To part in twain, that he might come and go.
But still the rising billows answered "No".
With that he stripped him to the ivory skin,
And crying, "Love I come," leapt lively in.
Whereat the sapphire-visag'd god[7] grew proud,
And made his capering Triton[8] sound aloud,
Imagining that Ganymede, displeas'd,
Had left the Heavens; therefore on him he seiz'd.
Leander striv'd, the waves about him wound,
And pulled him to the bottom, where the ground
Was strew'd with pearls, and in low coral groves
Sweet singing mermaids sported with their loves
On heaps of heavy gold, and took great pleasure
To spurn in careless sport the shipwrack treasure.
For here the stately azure palace stood,
Where kingly Neptune and his train abode.
The lusty god embraced him, called him "love",
And swore he never should return to Jove.
But when he knew it was not Ganymede,
For under water he was almost dead,
He heav'd him up, and looking on his face,
Beat down the bold waves with his triple mace,
Which mounted up, intending to have kiss'd him,
And fell in drops like tears because they miss'd him.
Leander being up, began to swim,
And looking back saw Neptune follow him;
Whereat aghast, the poor soul 'gan to cry,
"O let me visit Hero ere I die."
The god put Helle's bracelet on his arm,
And swore the sea should never do him harm.
He clapped his plump cheeks, with his tresses play'd,
And smiling wantonly, his love bewray'd[9]
He watched his arms, and as they open'd wide,
At every stroke, betwixt them would he slide,
And steal a kiss, and then run out and dance,
And as he turn'd, cast many a lustful glance,

And throw him gaudy toys to catch his eye,
And dive into the water, and there pry
Upon his breast, his thighs, and every limb,
And up again, and close beside him swim,
And talk of love. Leander made reply,
"You are deceiv'd; I am no woman, I".
Thereat smiled Neptune, and then told a tale,
How that a shepherd sitting in a vale
Played with a boy so lovely fair and kind, [10]
As for his love both earth and heaven pin'd;
That of the cooling river durst not drink,
Lest water nymphs should pull him from the brink.
And when he sported in the fragrant lawns,
Goat-footed Satyrs and upstarting Fauns
Would steal him thence. Ere half his tale was done,
"Aye me", Leander cried, "th' enamored sun,
That should now shine on Thetis' glassy bower,
Descends upon my radiant Hero's tower:
O that these tardy arms of mine were wings!"
And as he spake, upon the waves he springs.
Neptune was angry that he gave no ear,
And in his heart revenging malice bare:
He flung at him his mace, but as it went
He call'd it in, for love made him repent.
The mace returning back his own hand hit,
As meaning to be 'veng'd for darting it.
When this fresh bleeding wound Leander viewed,
His colour went and came, as if he rued
The grief which Neptune felt. In gentle breasts
Relenting thoughts, remorse and pity rests.
And who have hard hearts, and obdurate minds,
But vicious, hare-brained and illit'rate hinds?
The god seeing him with pity to be moved,
Thereon concluded that he was beloved.
(Love is too full of faith, too credulous,
With folly and false hopes deluding us.)
Wherefore, Leander's fancy to surprise,
To the rich Ocean for gifts he flies:

'Tis wisdom to give much, a gift prevails,
When deep persuading oratory fails....

(1598)

The Passionate Shepherd To His Love[11]
[Reconstruction of original four-stanza lyric]

Come live with me, and be my love,
And we will all the pleasures prove,
That Valleys, groves, hills, and fields,
Woods, or steepy mountain yields.

And we will sit upon the Rocks,
Seeing the Shepherds feed their flocks,
By shallow Rivers, to whose falls,
Melodious birds sing Madrigals.

And I will make thee beds of Rosies,
And a thousand fragrant posies,
A cap of flowers, and a kirtle,[12]
Embroid'red all with leaves of Myrtle.

A belt of straw, and Ivy buds,
With Coral clasps and Amber studs,
And if these things thy mind may move,
Then live with me, and be my love.

1 See Shakespeare's Sonnet 86, above.

2 Today it seems ironic that the Elegies were the target of the church's
wrath, as they are completely and overtly heterosexual in form and content,
while some of Marlowe's other works, which dealt explicitly with pedo-
philia and gay sex, were ignored by the book burners.

3 Colchas was an ancient country bordering on The Black Sea; it was there
that Jason and the Argonauts sought the Golden Fleece.

4 i.e., Narcissus; see Ovid and others, above.

---

5 Like Adonis, he preferred hunting to loving.

6 Thrace, an ancient country comprising much of modern Greece and Turkey.

7 Poseidon, the Greek god of the sea; known to the Romans as Neptune.

8 a son of Poseidon, a demigod of the sea with the torso of a man and the tail of a fish.

9 unclear; possibly "betray'd", or "array'd".

10 See "The Passionate Shepherd To His Love", below.

11 This poem has been referenced, copied, imitated, and parodied more than any other poem in the English language.

12 a kirtle refers to a tunic or coat worn by men especially in the Middle Ages; later, a long gown or dress worn by women. It can be argued that, in Marlowe's time, kirtle referred to a man's shirt.

APPENDIX

Biblical Variations

1 Samuel 20:41

In researching this text, I consulted a library shelf full of English-language translations of the Bible, a representative sample of which is presented below. Most used the *King James Version* as their English source.

While most editions attempt to minimalize the intensity and nature of David and Jonathan's passion, the bias and literary integrity of the translators is particularly evident regarding the lovers' kiss.[1] The strict scholastic notations of *The Anchor Bible* are interesting, though not very illuminating. On the whole, the passage remains mysterious and intriguing.

The sequence of events appears to have been this: the men meet for what will be the last time, kiss, weep together, and then *something* happens to David. That *something* is variously described as "exceeded", "recovered himself", "magnified", "was overcome", "there was no staunching David's tears", and "exerted himself". Among the myriad translations of the Bible into English, there is no consensus of opinion.

An interesting consideration here is the source of this information: since both Jonathan and Saul are long dead by the time that this account was written, we must assume that, if accurate, these facts could only have come from King David himself.

The simple fact that such a diversity of opinion (and outright deletion of the troublesome last part, in a quarter of the texts sampled above) occurs around this passage indicates that something is being said here which modern translators either cannot, or will not, easily render into English.

The Anchor Bible: "…Then they kissed each other and wept over each other […?…]" (note: at the end of the verse MT has 'd dwd hgdyl, "until David magnified [?]"…no easy translation emerges…Perhaps "unto weeping greatly").

Holy Bible: "…And both kissed as friends, and both wept as friends, until David was overcome."

KJV: "…And they kissed one another, and wept one with another, until David exceeded."

Knox's Old Testament translation from the Vulgate Latin: "…and they kissed one another and wept together; there was no staunching David's tears."

The Living Bible: "…they sadly shook hands, tears running down their cheeks until they could weep no more." (footnote: "Literally, 'David…bowed himself three times and they kissed each other and wept until David exceeded.')"

New American Bible: "…They kissed each other and wept aloud together."

New American Standard: "…And they kissed each other and wept together, but David more."

New Jerusalem Bible: "…Then they embraced each other, both weeping copiously."

New Oxford Bible: "…and they kissed each other and wept with each other; David wept the more. (note: Vulgate Heb. uncertain)"

New Scoffield Bible: "…and they kissed one another and wept one with another, until David |controlled himself| (note: exceeded)."

Revised Standard Version: "…and they kissed one another, and wept with one another, until David recovered himself. (note: or *exceeded*)"

Tyndale's Old Testament. : "…And they kissed each other and wept together, but David more abundantly."

Young's Literal Translation of the Bible: "…and they kiss one another, and they weep one with another, till David exerted himself."

Thomas Bulfinch
Straightening Up The Classics
(1796-1867 CE)

The cult of Puritanism runs deep in America, and aversion to gay sex seems to head the list of its attendant sexual phobias. Often, American literature reflects this cultural prudishness, leading to gross distortions in translations of more liberal texts. An important example of this is Bullfinch's 1855 *Mythology*,[1] a translation into English of several classical and medieval authors, including the Roman poet, Ovid. While faithfully translating most of the facts (and all of the heterosexual activity), Bulfinch systematically downplays and omits evidence of gay sexuality whenever he encounters it in these stories. The resulting bowdlerized texts have been widely used in the United States in place of the racier originals; Bulfinch has provided anti-sexual prudes with sanitized classical material for almost a century and a half.

Bulfinch's deliberate concealment of gay love is, unfortunately, the rule rather than the exception in the pre-Stonewall literature of this country. Over and over again, all pro-gay references are expunged from text books and library materials where young gays might find them. This deliberate castration of all gay love in English translations of classical material has a devastating effect on the gay psyche: denied access to our rich cultural heritage, all but the most diligent readers are presented with a bleak and wholly heterosexual literary landscape, a far cry from the rich pan-sexual tradition available to our European cousins.[2]

The brief excerpts offered here are intended to illustrate this defect in Bulfinch's recapitulation of Ovid's poetry.

from *The Age Of Fable:*

Hebe and Ganymede

Hebe, the daughter of Juno, and goddess of youth, was cup-bearer to the gods. The usual story is that she resigned her office on becoming the wife of Hercules.[3] But there is another statement. According to this, Hebe was dismissed from her office in consequence of a fall which she met with one day while in attendance on the gods. Her successor was Ganymede, a Trojan boy, whom Jupiter, in the disguise of an eagle, seized and carried off from the midst of his playfellows on Mount Ida, bore up to heaven, and installed in the vacant place....

Apollo and Hyacinthus

Apollo was passionately fond of a youth named Hyacinthus...and neglected for him his lyre and his arrows....[4]

Narcissus

Narcissus' cruelty in [the case of the nymph Echo] was not the only instance. He shunned all the rest of the nymphs, as he had done poor Echo. One day a maiden[5] who had endeavored in vain to attract him uttered a prayer that he might some time or other feel what it was to love and meet no return of affection. The avenging goddess heard and granted the prayer.

There was a clear fountain, with water like silver...hither came one day the youth, fatigued with hunting, heated and thirsty. He stooped down to drink, and saw his own image in the water; he thought it was some beautiful water-spirit living in the fountain.[6] He stood gazing with admiration at those bright eyes, those locks curled like the locks of Bacchus or Apollo, the rounded cheeks, the ivory neck, the parted lips, and the glow of health and exercise over all. He fell in love with himself. He brought his lips near to take a kiss; he plunged his arms in to embrace the beloved object. It fled at the touch, but returned again after a moment and renewed the fascination. He could not tear himself away; he lost all thought of food or rest, while he hovered over the edge of the fountain gazing upon his own image.

He talked with the supposed spirit: "Why, beautiful being, do you shun me? Surely my face is not one to repel you. The nymphs love me, and you yourself look not indifferent upon me. When I stretch forth my arms, you do the same; and you smile upon me and answer my beckonings with the like."

His tears fell into the water and disturbed the image....he cherished the flame that consumed him, so that by degrees he...pined away and died....

1 Originally published in three separate volumes, The Age of Fable (1855), The Age of Chivalry (1858), and Legends of Charlemagne (1863), the works have since been abridged by Edmund Fuller and published as one volume, entitled simply Mythology.

2 When examining any modern (post-industrial) translation of classical lore for homophobic distortion, the story of Ganymede is an excellent acid test for anti-gay bias; Bulfinch is no exception here. Books of quotes, encyclopedias, dictionaries, and other resource books also fall prey to obvious factual distortion when dealing with the Trojan boy-toy.

3 In classical lore, the demigod Hercules is associated with legions of male lovers; after he is immortalized, he is married off to Hebe.

4 The remainder of the tale is nearly word for word from Ovid's account, sans nudity.

5 Compare this to Ovid: "...finally one rejected youth, in prayer,/ Raised up his hands to Heaven: "May Narcissus/ Love one day, so, himself, and not win over/ The creature whom he loves!" Nemesis heard him...and judged the plea was righteous...."

6 This is unsupportable from Ovid's account; the water spirit idea is Bulfinch's own invention.

III.　　Timeline

3500	Egyptians Occupy The Nile Valley
3200	Foundation Of Troy
2500	Stonehenge (?)
2300	Sack Of Troy By Aryans
1770	Abraham The Patriarch Leaves Ur
1600	Hebrews Enter Egypt
1300	Trojan War (?)
1190	Final Destruction Of Troy
1020	Samuel Establishes Royal House In Israel
1000	David And Jonathan
850	Homer
753	Foundation Of Rome
600	*Tao Teh Ching* Written
586	Jews Taken Captive To Babylon
483	Death Of Buddha
416	"Symposium On Love"
399	Execution Of Socrates
380	Plato's Academy Of Athens Founded
326	Death Of Alexander The Great
135	Greece Submits To Rome
44	Julius Caesar Murdered
31	Death Of Cleopatra And Antony
4	Birth Of Jesus
00	Common Era Reckoning Begins
29	Crucifixion Of Jesus
60	*Metamorphoses, Epigrams* Published
70	Destruction Of The Temple At Jerusalem

130	Death & Deification Of Antinous
323	Christianity Adopted As State Religion Of Rome
476	Fall Of The Roman Empire
500	Kama Sutra Developed In India
579	Justinian Closes Plato's Academy
800	Charlemagne Crowned Emperor Of The West
1066	Norman Conquest
1152	Eleanor Of Acquitaine Marries Henry II
1189	Richard The Lion-Hearted Crowned King Of England
1233	Medieval Inquisition Launched By Pope Celestine IV
1478	Spanish Inquisition Launched By Ferdinand And Isabella
1492	Jews Expelled From Spain By Ferdinand And Isabella
1503	Michaelangelo's *David*
1518	Martin Luther's 95 Theses
1558	Coronation Of Elizabeth I
1593	Death Of Christopher Marlowe
1792	Blake's *The Marriage Of Heaven And Hell* Published
1853	Bullfinch's *Age Of Fable*
1859	Darwin's *Evolution Of Species*
1895	Oscar Wilde Imprisoned For Sodomy

Bibliography

Boswell, John, Christianity, *Homosexuality and Social Tolerance*, University of Chicago Press, Illinois, 1980

Boswell, John, *Same-Sex Unions In Pre-Modern Europe*, Vintage Books / Random, 1994

Bulfinch, Thomas, *Mythology*, a modern abridgement by Edward Fuller, Dell Publishing, New York, 1959

Complete Kama Sutra, The: The First Unabridged Modern Translation of The Classic Indian Text by Vatsyayana, translated by Alain Daniélou, Park Street Press, Vermont, 1994

Daniélou, Alain, *Shiva and Dionysus*, translated by K. F. Hurry, East-West Publications, 1979, 1982

Dancing With Siva, Satguru Sivaya Subramuniyaswami, Himalayan Academy, 1992

Five Great Dialogues of Plato, translated by B. Jowett, edited by Louise Ropes Loomis, D. Van Nostrand Company, Princeton, New Jersey, 1942

Guiding Light of Lao-Tzu: A New Translation and Commentary on the Tao Teh Ching, Henry Wei, Quest Books, Illinois, 1982

Iliad of Homer, The, translated with an introduction by Richard Lattimore, Phoenix Books, Chicago, 1951

Iliad, The, translated by Robert Fitzgerald, Anchor Books, 1974

Lambert, Royston, *Beloved and God: The Story of Hadrian and Antinous*, Weidenfeld and Nicolson, London, 1984

Letters of Alcipron, Aelian, and Philostratus, The, with an English translation by Allen Rogers Benner, Harvard University Press

Martial: Epigrams, edited and translated by D. R. Shackleton Bailey, in three volumes, Harvard University Press, USA&UK, 1993

Ovid: Metamorphoses, translated by Rolfe Humphries, Dana University Press, Bloomington, 1960

Spencer, Colin, *Homosexuality in History*, Harcourt Brace & Co., San Diego, 1995

Williamson, Marianne, *A Return To Love*, HarperCollins, New York, 1992

Yarbro, Chelsea Quinn, *Messages from Michael*, Berkely Books, 1979

ORDER FORM

Please send _____ copies of "Gay Testaments: Old and New" to the address below.

I have enclosed $12.95 per copy, plus $2.50 postage and handling for one copy ($4.00 total for two to five copies), in check or money order. (CA residents: please add $1.00 sales tax per copy.)

Name_____

Address_____

City_____State_____Zip code_____

Please copy or detach this page and mail with payment to:

Wind-Up Publications
2828 University Ave., 103#121
San Diego, CA 92104

Allow 4-6 weeks for delivery.
We appreciate the comments of our readers.

_____

_____

_____

_____